STUDENT DIGITAL MATERIALS

™

Boost students' learning with Class Booster! Fun games and activities motivate them to learn outside the classroom at their own pace. Automatic feedback builds their confidence with key vocabulary. The easy-to-use class management system tracks their activity and progress and sends reports. Get the most out of your classes with Class Booster!

Features for **Students**

Anytime, anywhere
Use on PC or mobile devices.

Talk or touch to answer
Get extra practice speaking.

* For select books with mobile app.

Collect stars, grow your avatar
Hatch your egg and watch it grow.

Simple, fun activities
Get extra practice before and after class with fun games and activities. No sign-in required.

Word Flash

Word Match

Unscramble

Quiz

* Different activities may be available.

Features for **Teachers**

Track student progress
Easy-to-use LMS sends student reports. Students only enter teacher's email address.

Activities

Comprehension

Top Students

How to access **Class Booster**

PC
Use the CD (with select books) or download from classbooster.net.

Mobile / Tablet
Search for the name of the book on Google Play or the Apple App Store, or scan the QR code on the back cover.

READING FOR SPEED AND FLUENCY SECOND EDITION 3

Paul Nation · Marcos Benevides · James Broadbridge · Joseph Siegel

© 2018 Compass Publishing

Managing Editor: Jon Edwards
Content Editor: Marcos Benevides
Proofreader: Jon Edwards
Cover/Interior Design: Lani Kim
Contributing Writers: Christopher Campbell, Paul Edmunds,
Moraig Macgillivray, Casey Malarcher, Jenna Myers, Dawn Nordquist,
Pierre Stapley, Adam Worcester, Patrick Yancey

email: info@compasspub.com
http://www.compasspub.com

ISBN 978-1-64015-069-0

11 10 9 8 7 6 5 4 3 2 1
22 21 20 19 18

Photo Credits

Pg. 39, Photo by Ian Lambot via Wikipedia Commons (CC BY-SA 4.0);
All other images © Shutterstock, Inc.

Printed in Korea

TABLE OF CONTENTS

INTRODUCTION

Why is it good to read faster?

Most learners of English read quite slowly—often less than 100 words per minute. They can easily read much faster if they read passages at the right level and if they have some practice in reading faster. This series of books will help you do this.

Why is it good to read faster? When you can read faster, you will find it easier to understand. You do not spend your time sounding out words, so you can give more time to understanding. When you read faster, you can read more. And reading is more fun when you can do it easily at a good speed.

There are many kinds of reading: reading for study, reading for fun, reading to learn about the world (such as reading newspapers), and reading to follow instructions. When you become faster at one kind of reading, you will also be faster at other kinds of reading too.

You may also be able to listen a bit faster because you are used to understanding English at a faster speed.

About these books

Using these books is different from other ways of studying English. Usually, you meet new words and new pieces of grammar and try to learn them bit by bit. However, these books try to have almost no new things to learn. The purpose is to make you use what you already know and use it as well as you possibly can. This is called "becoming fluent." When you are fluent in a language, you can use what you know well. The goal of this book is to make you a fluent reader.

Most learners read slowly because they meet many unknown words in their reading. The passages in these books have been prepared so that there will be very few unknown words in them. First, the passages are written using familiar, useful vocabulary. Also, the passages are about familiar things. In addition, the passages are grouped into themes so that the four passages on the same theme will become easier as you read your way through them. The earlier passages will make the later ones more familiar. Last, difficult vocabulary is reviewed before you read the passages. These things are done so that you can read the passages quickly without meeting many unknown words.

Reading these passages should help you learn to read faster. All the passages in the book are exactly 200 words long, and they are written largely within a vocabulary of 500 words and all in the same style.

Using these books

Follow these steps when you use the books. Your teacher can help you with this.

Step 1: Fill in the charts at the beginning of each set of passages. Make sure you know these words well before you begin reading.

Step 2: Before reading each passage, look at the time or start a timer. If you are reading in class, the teacher will tell you when to begin.

Step 3: Read the passage as quickly as you can while trying to understand it.

Step 4: As soon as you finish reading, write down how many minutes and seconds it took you to read the passage.

Step 5: Turn the page and answer the questions. While you are answering them, do not look back at the passage.

Step 6: Check your answers to the questions.

Step 7: Write your speed and question score the Reading Speed Chart at the back of the book. Every passage in the book has the same number of words, so your reading time can tell you your reading speed.

Step 8: Look at your reading speed. You should try to read at around 250 words per minute. You may have to practice by reading many passages before you can get to this speed, but this should be your goal. When you read the next passage, try to go a little faster.

A few things to think about

Your goal is not to be the fastest reader in the world, but you should learn to read at a normal, comfortable speed. For most people, this is around 250 words per minute, but some people can read faster. Reading faster is only good if you also understand what you read. That is why there are questions after each story. If you get an answer wrong, that is not a problem. Your main goal is to read faster. You will check your own questions and measure your own speed. Of course, it would be easy to cheat if you wanted to. However, if you cheat, you know that your speed and question score is not really your score. Use these books honestly and properly, and with time, you will see your reading get better.

About the Authors

Paul Nation is Professor Emeritus in Applied Linguistics at the School of Linguistics and Applied Language Studies at Victoria University of Wellington, New Zealand. He has taught in Indonesia, Thailand, the United States, Finland, and Japan. His special interests are language teaching methodology and vocabulary learning. *Marcos Benevides* has written and edited many international award-winning books for language learners. He teaches at J. F. Oberlin University in Tokyo. *James Broadbridge* is a doctoral candidate in TESL, an award-nominated graded reader author, and a curriculum coordinator at J. F. Oberlin University. *Joseph Siegel* holds a PhD in Applied Linguistics and has researched various aspects of ELT. He teaches at Örebro University in Sweden.

1 | Nature

1. Are human beings animals? Why or why not?
2. What do you know about rainforests? What are they, and why are they important?
3. If all bees die, what will happen?

BRAZIL—A view from the air of the Amazon River winding through the Brazilian rainforest.

01 Humans

√	Keyword	Category	Definition	Use in a sentence
	zoo			
	two-legged			
	tools			
	language			French is known as 'the language of love'.
	stick	noun		
	clothing		what you wear to cover your body and keep warm	
	ability			
	feelings			
	angry			
	clearly			

02 Rainforests

√	Keyword	Category	Definition	Use in a sentence
	earth			
	centimeter			
	cover	noun		
	share	noun		
	leaves			
	two-thirds		66% of something	
	is worth	phrase		
	unfortunately			Unfortunately, it rained during the BBQ party.
	medicine			
	throw away			

03 The Hippo

✓	Keyword	Category	Definition	Use in a sentence
	truth		something that is a fact; not false	
	in fact			
	lion			
	protect			
	attack			
	up to			Some snakes can grow up to eight meters long.
	kilometer			
	kilogram			
	stick out	verb		
	breath	noun		

04 Bees

✓	Keyword	Category	Definition	Use in a sentence
	difficult			
	hurt			It hurts if you are hit by a ball.
	nature	noun		
	workers			
	grow			
	pick up			
	drop off		to leave something in a certain place	
	pollen			
	land	noun		
	favorite			

Humans

How are we different from animals?

There are many different kinds of animals at the zoo. However, the animal you will see the most does not live in the zoo. It is a tall two-legged animal called a human. We humans like to think that we are different from other animals. But why?

5　　One reason is our use of tools. While other animals use tools, none use them as much as we do. Animals may use sticks to get food and build a place to live, but we use thousands of special tools every day to make our lives easier and more comfortable. Cars, phones, and clothing are just some of the tools that help us in our everyday lives. Other animals cannot make such special tools.

10　　Language is another special human tool. While animals use simple calls to talk to each other, none can use language in the way that we can. For example, other animals cannot talk about tomorrow or about things you can't see. They cannot tell stories or learn from a book. Humans use language to do these things and more.

Another way in which we are different from other animals is our ability to 15　have many different feelings. Humans can feel happy, sad, angry, and many other feelings. Animals do not have as many feelings as humans, and their feelings are not like ours. For example, humans can have two or more feelings at once. When someone dies, we may feel sad, angry, and happy all 20　at the same time. Having these different feelings at the same time can make humans act in ways unlike other animals.

We humans like to think 25　that we are special—and clearly, in some ways, we are special. However, we are not that different either. Think about that the next time you 30　visit a zoo.

A Circle the right answer.

1. The main idea in this reading is:

    a. Humans are the most intelligent animals in the world.

    b. Human babies learn to use tools from their parents.

    c. Humans are different from other animals in some ways.

    d. Animals at the zoo often feel sad and angry.

According to the reading:

2. Humans are a kind of animal.	T	F
3. Humans are the only animals that use tools.	T	F
4. Some animals use language the same way humans do.	T	F
5. Some animals have feelings the same way humans do.	T	F

B Check your answers.

Score _____ /5

C Summarize the key points in the reading. Turn to page 17.

Expansion Questions

1. Have you been to a zoo? What animals did you see there?

_____

2. Can animals use tools? What are some examples?

_____

3. Do animals have feelings like humans?

_____

Rainforests

What are rainforests, and why are they important?

Rainforests are very thick, warm, and wet forests. They are usually found in the hottest parts of the earth and often have five hundred centimeters or more of rain each year. That's more than a centimeter of rain each day. Rainforests are also very rich in life. In fact, it seems that 40% to 75% of all living things began their life in rainforests.

The plants that grow in rainforests often grow very large. The thick leaves of the tallest trees keep out most of the sunlight, so inside a rainforest it can be very dark. Under this thick cover of trees, other plants must fight for their share of sunlight. Plants must grow very quickly and often on top of one another, making a thick cover of plants.

Along with lots of plants, rainforests are also home to many animals. Scientists think that rainforests are home to two-thirds of all the living plants and animals on earth, but in fact this number is just a guess. There is no way to actually count all of the living things in all of the rainforests of the world. Even now, scientists continue to discover new and unknown kinds of living things every year.

Although rainforests seem like wild and dangerous places, they are worth a lot to us. Not only do rainforests help to clean our air, scientists also think that 25% of all our natural medicines comes from plants and animals discovered in rainforests. And yet, less than 1% of total different living things in rainforests have been studied for their use in making medicines.

Unfortunately, not everyone agrees that rainforests are important. Since 1970, we have lost about 20% of the Amazon rainforest. Once they go, rainforests are gone forever. Sadly, we may never know what we are throwing away.

Time

A Circle the right answer.

1. The main idea in this reading is:
   a. Rainforests are important to life on earth.
   b. Rainforests are very hot and wet places.
   c. All our medicines come from rainforests.
   d. Rainforests are difficult places to live in.

According to the reading:

2. Scientists have finished counting all animals in rainforests.   T   F
3. Rainforests are worth a lot to humans.   T   F
4. Some rainforests are in cold, dry places.   T   F
5. The Amazon will be completely gone by 2050.   T   F

B Check your answers.

Score _____ /5

C Summarize the key points in the reading. Turn to page 17.

Expansion Questions

1. Are there any rainforests in your country?
   _____

2. Have you ever visited a forest or a rainforest? Describe it.
   _____

3. What can we do to save natural areas such as rainforests?
   _____

The Hippo

Are hippos really dangerous?

Most people's idea of the hippo is of a large, slow, friendly-looking animal. This, however, is a long way from the truth. In fact, the hippopotamus (meaning "river horse") is one of the most dangerous animals in all of Africa. They are even more dangerous than lions and kill more than five hundred people each year.

5   Hippos are dangerous because they will do anything to protect their living space and their young. If they feel they are being attacked, they become very dangerous. When they open their mouth wide, they are showing their teeth, so be careful.

Hippos are also surprisingly fast. They can run at up to 30 kilometers an hour,
10 which is faster than most humans. That's very fast when you consider that a hippo can be up to 3,200 kilograms.

Paul Templar is one man who knows how dangerous hippos are. He used to take visitors on trips down the Zambezi River. One day his boat was attacked by a hippo. The hippo held him in its mouth and took him to the bottom of the river.
15 The bottom part of Paul's body was in the hippo's mouth, while the top half of his body was sticking out. Paul held his breath and hoped the hippo would open its mouth and let him go. Then the hippo went back up for air, and Paul got free. His friend pulled him out of the river, and even though he was badly hurt,
20 Paul lived. He was very lucky.

We should all learn something from Paul's experience. The animals we see on television or in books often look nice or friendly, but the
25 truth can be quite different. Wild and unknown animals can be dangerous. If you are not careful, you may make a mistake that could kill you.

Time

A Circle the right answer.

1. The main idea in this reading is:
   a. Hippos live in the water.
   b. Hippos are dangerous animals.
   c. Hippos can eat anything.
   d. Hippo hunting is a problem in Africa.

According to the reading:

2. Hippos are more dangerous than lions.   T   F
3. Hippos open their mouth to show their teeth.   T   F
4. Hippos are very slow on land and get tired easily.   T   F
5. Paul Templar was killed by a hippo.   T   F

B Check your answers.

Score _____ /5

C Summarize the key points in the reading. Turn to page 17.

Expansion Questions

1. Have you ever seen a hippo in real life? Describe it.
   _____

2. What are the most dangerous animals in your country?
   _____

3. What advice would you give about avoiding a dangerous animal?
   _____

Bees

Why are we losing bees? Should we be worried?

Bees can be difficult to live with. When you are walking in a park on a nice day, you don't want a bee flying around you. Most people worry about
5 being hurt by a bee. It can hurt a lot and can even kill some people. However, bees are also an important part of nature. If all bees died at once, it could be a real problem for life on earth.

10 Bees are important for a number of reasons, but the most important reason for us is food. Many of the food plants we grow need bees to live. Like little workers, bees go from plant to plant,
15 picking up and dropping off small pieces of pollen. If there were no bees to do this, the pollen couldn't easily move from one plant to the next and new plants wouldn't be able to grow.

20 In some parts of the world, the number of bees has gone down in the past few years. Scientists are worried that we are killing the bees by putting too many bad things in the water and in the ground. Also, we may be using too much land for growing human food and not enough for the plants and flowers that the bees like. If we continue this way, we may lose not only bees, but many of our favorite
25 kinds of food too.

However, there is some good news. In a few places around the world, where beekeepers and other food growers have worked together to save the bees, the number of bees has started to go up again. The problem is that it takes more time and money to save bees than to do nothing. In other words, saving bees makes
30 the price of food go up, and nobody wants that to happen.

Time

A Circle the right answer.

1. The main idea in this reading is:

    a. Bees are dangerous to children.

    b. Bees are good at making honey.

    c. Bees can communicate by dancing.

    d. Bees are important for humans.

According to the reading:

2. Scientists want to protect us from bees.   T   F

3. The number of bees is going up too much.   T   F

4. In some countries, bees are a special food.   T   F

5. Bees in the United States stopped making honey.   T   F

B Check your answers.

Score _____ /5

C Summarize the key points in the reading. Turn to page 17.

Expansion Questions

1. Have you ever been stung by a bee? How did it feel?

_____

2. Do you know of any animals in your area that are endangered?

_____

3. Would you pay more for food if it helped to save endangered animals?

_____

SUMMARIZE »»»

Summarize the key points in the readings. Include the words in the box. You can look back at the text when you do this.

01 Humans

tools	language	special	feelings

_____

_____

_____

_____

02 Rainforests

plants	animals	air	medicine

_____

_____

_____

_____

03 The Hippo

protect	fast	dangerous	Paul Templar

_____

_____

_____

_____

04 Bees

important	food	land	save

_____

_____

_____

_____

2 People

1. Have you ever heard of Madonna? Who is she, and why is she famous?
2. Can you name some great athletes? What sport do they play, and what else do you know about them?
3. Have you ever read or seen a play by Shakespeare? Describe it.

MANNHEIM, GERMANY—A crowd enjoys a band's performance at

05 The Greatest of All Time

✓	Keyword	Category	Definition	Use in a sentence
	athlete			
	boxer			
	compare			
	within			
	for example			
	competition			
	even though			I had to walk to school even though it was raining.
	fewer			
	imagine		to picture something in your mind	
	judge	verb		

06 William Shakespeare

✓	Keyword	Category	Definition	Use in a sentence
	doubt			He's so busy today; I doubt he'll have time for lunch.
	play	noun		
	work	noun		
	available			
	effect			
	language			
	poem			
	quote		the use of someone else's words	
	pleasing	adjective		
	compare			

07 Madonna

✓	Keyword	Category	Definition	Use in a sentence
	stage			
	bestselling			
	smart			
	consider			
	prize		an award for good work	
	musical	noun		
	sexual			It's natural to have sexual feelings as you grow up.
	saint			
	image			
	magazine			

08 Women in Science

✓	Keyword	Category	Definition	Use in a sentence
	consider		to think deeply about a topic	
	involve	verb		
	deep			
	discovery			The discovery of DNA was important to science.
	Nobel Prize	proper noun		
	radiation			
	elements			
	DNA	noun (acronym)		
	studies	noun		
	field		an area of study	

The Greatest of All Time

Who is the greatest athlete ever? Track 05

The question of who is the greatest athlete of all time is a difficult one to answer. First of all, comparing athletes across different sports is almost impossible. Who can say that a boxer such as Mohammed Ali was a better or worse athlete than a top baseball player such as Ichiro Suzuki? Their sports are so different
5   that it is impossible to compare.

Comparing athletes within a single sport is a little easier, but even that can still lead to problems. In men's tennis, for example, Roger Federer is believed by many to be the greatest of all time. This is because he has won more competitions than any other tennis player. He passed the earlier winner, Pete Sampras, in 2009
10 when he won his fifteenth major competition.

However, does this mean that Federer is in fact the best? Many say that another tennis player, Rafa Nadal, is better—even though Nadal has not won as many major competitions. This is because he has beaten Federer many times; surely this makes him better than Federer.

15 Another interesting player to consider in men's tennis is the Australian player, Rod Laver. Laver only won eleven major competitions, which is fewer than Sampras, Nadal, or Federer. However, Laver won his eleven competitions even though he was stopped from playing for five years during his best years. It is easy to imagine that he would have won many more major competitions during
20 those five years, which could have made him the best.

Judging athletes is not a science. Some people will always want to support their favorite players, and
25 often who is "the greatest" will change when we think about different parts of their game. We may never agree who is the greatest of all time, but maybe that's
30 not a bad thing.

Time

A Circle the right answer.

1. The main idea in this reading is:

  a. Tennis is the greatest sport in the world.

  b. It's not easy to judge who is the best player.

  c. Rod Laver would have been the best player of all time.

  d. We need to have more competitions to know who is the best.

According to the reading:

2. Rafa Nadal is a tennis player.	T	F
3. Boxing is more difficult than baseball.	T	F
4. Federer, Nadal, and Laver are all good players.	T	F
5. Mohammed Ali also played professional baseball.	T	F

B Check your answers.

Score _____/5

C Summarize the key points in the reading. Turn to page 29.

Expansion Questions

1. Who is your country's greatest athlete?

_____

2. Do you know any great tennis players?

_____

3. Do you think it is possible to compare players across different sports?

_____

William Shakespeare

Who was Shakespeare, and why is he so important?

William Shakespeare is without a doubt the most important writer in English. His work is now available in all major languages, and his plays have been seen all over the world. The

5 ideas in his work have had a major effect on other writers. His words have even helped to change the English language itself.

We don't know much about Shakespeare's life. What we do know is that he

10 was born in 1564 in the small English town of Stratford-upon-Avon. When he was eighteen, he married a woman named Anne, and they had three children. In his early twenties, he worked in London as an actor and writer. He

15 became very successful.

Shakespeare stopped working in 1613, and he died in 1616.

We also know that, between around 1585 and 1615, Shakespeare wrote some of the best plays and poems in the English language. His best-known plays are *Hamlet, Othello, Romeo and Juliet, King Lear,* and *Macbeth.* Even if you have

20 never seen or read any of them, it is likely that you may still know some of the stories and quotes. For example, do you know the quote, "To be or not to be?"

Shakespeare's poems were very different from other writers' poems. For example, in one of his poems, Shakespeare surprises the reader by saying that his lover is not as beautiful as the sun and not as pleasing as music. It does not

25 seem like a love poem until the end. There, Shakespeare surprises us again by saying that his lover is more beautiful than any other woman who is compared to those things.

Today, we think of Shakespeare as 'difficult'. Although it's true that his language is a little hard to read now, you may be surprised that his ideas are as

30 fresh as ever.

Time _____

A Circle the right answer.

1. The main idea in this reading is:
    a. Shakespeare lived an exciting life.
    b. Some of Shakespeare's plays have been lost.
    c. Shakespeare's poems were his best work.
    d. Shakespeare is a very important writer.

According to the reading:

2. Shakespeare's ideas are still important today.   T   F
3. Shakespeare was successful during his life.   T   F
4. Shakespeare never got married or had children.   T   F
5. Shakespeare wrote both plays and poems.   T   F

B Check your answers.

Score _____/5

C Summarize the key points in the reading. Turn to page 29.

Expansion Questions

1. Who is your favorite author? What do you know about his or her life?
   _____

2. Do you know about Shakespeare? How many of his plays can you name?
   _____

3. What is the most important story in your country's literature?
   _____

Madonna

Why is Madonna so famous?

Madonna Louise Ciccone, known on stage only by her first name, was one of the greatest pop stars of the late 1900s and early 2000s. She became well known in the 1980's for her bestselling pop songs, such as *Material Girl* and *Like a Virgin*. However, unlike most pop singers, Madonna was also a very smart business person,
5 songwriter, book writer, and actor.

As an actor, Madonna starred in several big movies and was even considered for a best actress prize for her part in the 1996 musical *Evita*. As a writer, she wrote bestselling children's books and coffee-table books. In 2004, she was called "America's smartest business woman" by a professor at a top business university.

10 Madonna is well known not only for her art and business sense, but also for being different. As a young rising star, Madonna did many things which made older people unhappy and uncomfortable but which helped her to become well known. For example, she started wearing underwear on top of her clothes, she put Christian ideas into her music and videos, and she lived a sexually open
15 life. In the song *Like a Prayer*, for example, Madonna puts a Christian idea together with sexual ideas. To the listener, it's not clear if the song is sung to God or to a lover. The video for the song also made people uncomfortable by showing Madonna kissing a saint.

Madonna's love life only
20 added to her "bad girl" image. She married three times: to actors Sean Penn and Warren Beatty, and to filmmaker Guy Ritchie. She also dated basketball star
25 Dennis Rodman and troubled artist Jean-Michel Basquiat, among others.

In 2011, music magazine Rolling Stone called Madonna
30 the 36ᵗʰ greatest artist of all time, ahead of such well-known singers as John Lennon, David Bowie, and Jim Morrison.

Time _____

A Circle the right answer.

1. The main idea in this reading is:

    a. Madonna always wrote her own music and books.

    b. Madonna is the world's smartest business woman.

    c. Madonna is well known for many reasons, not only for her music.

    d. Madonna's unusual love life caused many problems.

According to the reading:

2. Madonna was a successful writer of books.		T	F
3. Madonna was once married to Tom Cruise.		T	F
4. Madonna's songs made some people uncomfortable.		T	F
5. Rolling Stone has called her the best artist of all time.		T	F

B Check your answers.

Score _____/5

C Summarize the key points in the reading. Turn to page 29.

Expansion Questions

1. Who is the biggest pop star in the world today?

_____

2. Can you think of another person who is famous in different fields, like Madonna?

_____

3. Should fans care about the unusual personal life of a star?

_____

Women in Science

Are there enough women working in scientific fields?

Not so long ago, science was considered too dangerous and too difficult for women. People used to tell women that they
5 should stay at home and look after their family. Most people at the time believed that science and other work which involved deep thinking was for men,
10 not for women. However, some women scientists did go on to do very important work.

When people think of well-known women scientists,
15 Marie Curie is always at the top of the list. Curie (1867 - 1934) was the first woman to win a Nobel Prize and the only woman ever to win two. She won the prizes because of her work on radiation and her discovery of two new elements.

However, Marie Curie is not the only woman in her family to do important work in the world of science. Her daughter, Irene Joliot-Curie (1897 - 1956), also
20 won a Nobel Prize. Together, the Curies are the first mother-and-daughter winners of Nobel Prizes.

Rosalind Franklin (1920 - 1958) is another woman who won a Nobel Prize. Without her work on DNA, much of the recent work would not have been possible. However, like the Curies, when Franklin started her studies, science was something
25 mostly done by men. At first, even Franklin's own father did not want her to go into science.

Many other now well-known scientists, such as Lise Meitner, another scientist in the same field as Curie, were stopped from studying as young women. Yet, they went on to make important discoveries which have helped us all. If you want to
30 do something, you should not let others stop you.

In most countries, women make up about 50% of the people. It is strange to imagine how much better the world could be today if we had always helped both men and women to study science.

Time _____

A Circle the right answer.

1. The main idea in this reading is:

    a. There have been many successful women scientists.

    b. Scientists sometimes study with their family members.

    c. Very few Nobel Prize winners have been women.

    d. Marie Curie is the best-known woman in science

According to the reading:

2. In the past, science was too difficult for women.	T	F
3. Marie Curie was the only scientist in her family.	T	F
4. Rosalind Franklin's father wanted her to become a scientist.	T	F
5. About 50% of scientists today are women.	T	F

B Check your answers.

Score _____/5

C Summarize the key points in the reading. Turn to page 29.

Expansion Questions

1. Who is the best-known scientist alive today? What do they study?

_____

2. Can you think of some other well-known scientists? How many are women?

_____

3. Are men and women different in scientific ability? How?

_____

SUMMARIZE ⟫⟫

Summarize the key points in the readings. Include the words in the box. You can look back at the text when you do this.

05 The Greatest of All Time

compare	tennis	beat	competitions

_____

_____

_____

_____

06 William Shakespeare

important	life	plays	poems

_____

_____

_____

_____

07 Madonna

pop star	actor	different	image

_____

_____

_____

_____

08 Women in Science

important	Nobel Prize	Rosalind Franklin	discoveries

_____

_____

_____

_____

CHAPTER

3 Places

1. What place in your country is the most famous? Why?
2. Are there parts of your city that are too crowded? If so, what should be done about them?
3. What do you know about Easter Island? What is it famous for?

DUNHUANG, CHINA—Camels carry tourists across a section of the Silk Road that passes through the desert in Gansu province, Western China.

09 Easter Island

✓	Keyword	Category	Definition	Use in a sentence
	except			
	mysterious			
	Pacific Ocean	proper noun		
	statues			
	moai			The moai on Easter Island face toward the sea.
	story		one floor of a building	
	builders			
	honor	verb		
	past			
	notice			

10 The Dead Sea

✓	Keyword	Category	Definition	Use in a sentence
	lowest			
	surface		the outer or top layer of something	
	sea level			
	salt			These potato chips have too much salt.
	future			
	valley			
	Mediterranean			
	lake			
	mix	verb		
	pipe	noun		

11 The Silk Road

✓	Keyword	Category	Definition	Use in a sentence
	silk			
	collection			
	the West	proper noun		
	the East			
	cloth			
	is valued			Gold is valued by people around the world.
	magical			
	culture			
	religion			
	the Black Death		a deadly disease; the bubonic plague	

12 Kowloon Walled City

✓	Keyword	Category	Definition	Use in a sentence
	Hong Kong			
	destroy			
	densely			
	populated	adjective		
	football field			
	floor		one story of a building	
	laws			
	crime			Drunk driving is a crime in most countries.
	ordinary			
	illegal			

Easter Island

How were these unusual statues made, and why? Track 09

The earth is full of interesting places. One such place is an island 4,000 kilometers west of South America called Easter Island. Except for some smaller islands around it, there is no other land for hundreds of kilometers anywhere near Easter Island.

One of the things that make Easter Island so mysterious is that it is not like
5 any other island in the south Pacific Ocean. The island is mostly grassy fields, with no forests or rivers. In fact, it does not have any large plants or trees at all. All other large Pacific islands, such as Tahiti, have many rivers and forests.

However, what makes Easter Island stand out are its hundreds of well-known very large stone statues of people. These statues are called moai, and they were
10 a mystery for a long time. By the time Europeans arrived in 1722, the people of Easter Island had forgotten how and why the moai were made.

There are more than 800 large moai on the island. Some are just one meter tall, while others are over ten meters tall. That's as tall as a three-story building. How did the builders make and move such heavy things, and why did they do it?

15 After many years of study, scientists can now answer the first question. The
moai were made in one place on
the island and then moved by
rolling them over hundreds of
cut trees. Hundreds of years ago,
20 Easter Island was covered with
trees, but these were cut down to
make and move the moai.

Today, the question about
Easter Island is not how the moai
25 were made, but why? Did the
people there make them to honor
people from their past or for
another reason? More importantly,
did they not notice what they
30 were doing to their island?

Time _____

A Circle the right answer.

1. The main idea in this reading is:

   a. Easter Island is a well-known vacation spot.

   b. The beaches on Easter Island are the best in the Pacific.

   c. Many years ago, Easter Island was a powerful country.

   d. Easter Island is an interesting and unusual place.

According to the reading:

2.	No one knows who made the moai statues.	T	F
3.	Hundreds of years ago, Easter Island had many trees.	T	F
4.	Some of the moai statues are made of wood.	T	F
5.	Hawaii and Tahiti also have moai statues.	T	F

B Check your answers.

Score _____ /5

C Summarize the key points in the reading. Turn to page 41.

Expansion Questions

1. What do you know about Easter Island?

_____

2. Have you ever been to an island far away from the mainland?

_____

3. Are there any old and mysterious objects in your country?

_____

The Dead Sea

What makes this place unusual?

The Dead Sea is the lowest point on the surface of the earth. It is 418 meters below sea
5   level. Although called a "sea," it is actually a saltwater lake between Jordan, Israel, and the West Bank of Palestine.
10   The Dead Sea has been a part of human history for thousands of years, but it may not be there in the future if we cannot save it.
15   The Dead Sea got its name because it is so salty that animals and plants cannot live in it. Its waters are made up of about 30% salt, which is more than eight times saltier than the earth's seas. However, this high amount of salt can make it fun for visitors, who can enjoy lying on top of
20   the water without going under.

The Dead Sea is in the middle of a deep valley. This valley is over 6,000 km long, running from Turkey to Africa. Around three million years ago, the area used to get filled by the Mediterranean Sea, making a large saltwater lake. Around two million years ago, the land moved and stopped it from mixing with
25   the Mediterranean. This made the saltwater lake become smaller and saltier over time. Around 10,000 years ago, it reached the size it is today.

Today, the Dead Sea gets only 50 mm of rain each year. The Jordan River is the only river which feeds it. Unfortunately, in recent years, people have taken a lot of water from the Jordan River to drink and grow food. This means that the
30   Dead Sea is getting even less fresh water.

People in the area have started trying to save the Dead Sea. For example, Jordan, with help from Israel and Palestine, is now building a pipe to bring in water from the Red Sea.

Circle the right answer.

1. The main idea in this reading is:

   a. The area around the Dead Sea has many beautiful beaches.

   b. The Dead Sea has a long history, but its future is in danger.

   c. Fish and sea plants cannot live in the Dead Sea.

   d. Many countries take water from the Dead Sea.

According to the reading:

2.	The Dead Sea is in Jordan.	T	F
3.	No one knows how the Dead Sea got its name.	T	F
4.	The Dead Sea is not really a sea but a big lake.	T	F
5.	The Dead Sea is getting less water every year.	T	F

B Check your answers.

Score _____/5

C Summarize the key points in the reading. Turn to page 41.

Expansion Questions

1. Why do you think the Dead Sea has this unusual name?

   _____

2. Have you ever been to a big lake? How is it different from the sea?

   _____

3. Can you think of other places on earth where few animals can live?

   _____

The Silk Road

What is the Silk Road, and what was it used for?

The Silk Road is not really one single road. It is a collection of ways—by land and by sea—that joined the West and the East more than 2,000 years ago. The Silk Road was first made around 120 BC in China and ran all the way to the Mediterranean Sea.

5   It is called the Silk Road because silk was the most important thing to be carried and sold. At the time, silk was only made in China. This beautiful cloth was highly valued by rich people all over Europe. Silk is light, yet also strong and warm. To Europeans, it was almost magical.

   Once it first came to Europe, rich people there wanted more and more silk.
10 The movement of goods to and from China and the West grew quickly, as sellers travelled there and back again for thousands of kilometers. They carried silk and tea from China; they took European gold, valuable stones, and glass when they went the other way.

   The Silk Road brought great change to the world. As different countries met,
15 ideas moved from person to person, and cultures started to change. One example is the movement of religion. Buddhism, which began in India, moved to China, Korea, Japan, and Central Asia at that time.

   The Silk Road also brought death to millions of people. New illnesses travelled across Asia and Europe along with the travelers. One of the deadliest was the
20 Black Death. This killed more than 100 million people in Europe and Asia—about 20% of the world's people at that time.

   The Silk Road brought many great things to the world. Many people became rich, and
25 people's lives changed. However, like any change, it also brought unhappiness. Now China has started rebuilding the Silk Road.
30 What changes will that bring?

(Time)

A Circle the right answer.

1. The main idea in this reading is:
   a. The Silk Road brought many changes to the world.
   b. China is now trying to rebuild the Silk Road.
   c. The East and the West have always been connected.
   d. The Silk Road brought many Eastern ideas to the West.

According to the reading:

2. The Black Death killed many people in Europe.   T   F
3. Europeans had too much silk, so they sold it to China.   T   F
4. The Silk Road is one single big road from China to Rome.   T   F
5. The Silk Road carried goods, ideas, and also diseases.   T   F

B Check your answers.

Score _____/5

C Summarize the key points in the reading. Turn to page 41.

Expansion Questions

1. What are the top goods that are made in your country?
   _____

2. What's your favorite item that is made in another country?
   _____

3. What part of your culture is well known in other countries?
   _____

Kowloon Walled City

Why was this city destroyed? Track 12

In 1993, the government of Hong Kong destroyed an area known as the Kowloon Walled City. This small part of Hong Kong
5 was the most densely populated place on earth. By 1990, more than 50,000 people lived inside an area of 26,000 m². That's about the same size as four football fields.

10 People lived in tall buildings that were up to fourteen stories high. These buildings grew from year to year. If there was no space, people would simply build another
15 floor on top. The buildings were poorly made, unsafe, and so close together that almost no sunlight reached the ground.

Photo by Ian Lambot via Wikipedia Commons (CC BY-SA 4.0)

Most of the people who lived in the Kowloon Walled City were poor, and the
20 area was known for being dangerous. Because it was difficult for the police to enter, people there often did not follow the laws of Hong Kong. There were drugs, crime, and sex workers. Many outsiders were afraid to go there at night.

However, most people who lived there were not bad people. Most were ordinary people trying to live. Many had come from other parts of China and
25 just wanted to work hard and feed their families. Inside the city, there were small businesses such as stores and food shops. There were also many illegal doctors and dentists. It was a difficult life, but for many people, it was home.

After the Kowloon Walled City was destroyed, the government of Hong Kong built a beautiful park in its place. Most people were happy to see the end
30 of such an unhealthy, dirty, dangerous place. However, for many of the people who lived there, there was also sadness. The Kowloon Walled City was where they had grown up with their friends and family. For these people, it was the end of a way of life.

Time

A Circle the right answer.

1. The main idea in this reading is:
   a. Kowloon Walled City was originally part of China.
   b. Hong Kong is a very densely populated place.
   c. Hong Kong was wrong to take down Kowloon Walled City.
   d. Kowloon Walled City was taken down for good reasons, but it was home to many people.

According to the reading:

2. Outsiders were afraid to go to Kowloon Walled City.   T   F
3. The walled city was small but safe and comfortable.   T   F
4. Most people in the walled city were bad people.   T   F
5. Today, Kowloon is a modern shopping mall.   T   F

B Check your answers.

Score _____ /5

C Summarize the key points in the reading. Turn to page 41.

Expansion Questions

1. What's the most crowded place you know? What is it like?

   _____

2. Are there parts of your city that are dangerous to visit?

   _____

3. How would you feel if you were forced to move to a new home?

   _____

SUMMARIZE

Summarize the key points in the readings. Include the words in the box. You can look back at the text when you do this.

09 | Easter Island

mysterious	plants or trees	rolling	moai

_____

_____

_____

_____

10 | The Dead Sea

mysterious	plants or trees	rolling	moai

_____

_____

_____

_____

11 | The Silk Road

joined	change	illnesses	silk

_____

_____

_____

_____

12 | Kowloon Walled City

densely populated	dangerous	park	destroyed

_____

_____

_____

_____

1. Is there a lot of street art in your city? If so, what is your opinion of it?

2. What is your favorite English children's book? Why?

3. What is the most famous song ever written? Who wrote it?

FRANCE—A wall is covered with street art of a bridge and buildings.

13 The Happy Birthday Song

✓	Keyword	Category	Definition	Use in a sentence
	history			
	lyrics			
	include			
	company			
	deal	noun		
	law			
	public			
	ad			
	worldwide			This credit card can be used worldwide.
	hit		a song, movie, etc. which is very successful	

14 Harry Potter

✓	Keyword	Category	Definition	Use in a sentence
	series			Harry Potter is a well-known book series.
	bestselling	adjective		
	reject			
	accept			
	magic	noun		
	wizard		a person who uses magic	
	mention			
	argue			
	success			
	countless	adjective		

15 Alice in Wonderland

✓	Keyword	Category	Definition	Use in a sentence
	adventures	noun		
	wonderland			
	rabbit			
	unusual			
	Thames River			
	character		a person in a story, movie, etc.	
	suggest			
	collection			
	mathematics			Mathematics is the study of numbers.
	puzzle	noun		

16 Street Art

✓	Keyword	Category	Definition	Use in a sentence
	vandalism			
	ancient			
	prehistoric			
	spray paint			Use spray paint to fix that scratch on your car.
	damage	verb		
	property			
	Banksy	proper noun		
	sharp			
	airstrike			
	remove		to take something away	

The Happy Birthday Song

Who wrote this popular song?

Happy Birthday is a short song with a long and interesting history. Today it is one of the most loved songs in English. However, did you know that this song was written with a different name and for a very different reason?

Nobody knows who wrote the lyrics for *Happy Birthday*, but the music was
5 written by two American teachers, Mildred and Patty Hill. In 1893, Mildred wrote the well-known song, and her sister Patty added some simple words. They called their new song *Good Morning to All*. They used it to begin class each day: "Good morning to you / good morning to you / good morning dear children / good morning to all."

10 The Hill sisters put *Good Morning to All* in a song book in 1893. Thirty-one years later, a man named Robert Coleman included it in another song book, with the lyrics changed to "happy birthday to you." No one knows who wrote the

new words, but the song quickly
became used at birthday par-
15 ties. Soon, businesses started
using the song as well.

In 1935, another Hill sister,
Jessica, asked a music company
to help protect the music to
20 *Happy Birthday*. The music
company made a deal so that no
one could sing Happy Birthday
for money without asking them
first. This deal is still in law. We
25 can sing *Happy Birthday* to our
family and friends, but we can't

sing the song in public or use it in something that makes money, such as a movie or an ad.

Today, the music company still owns *Happy Birthday*. Each year, the song
30 brings in about two million dollars. Half of that money goes to the music company and half to the family of the Hill sisters. Their simple classroom song has become a worldwide hit.

Time _____

A Circle the right answer.

1. The main idea in this reading is:

    a. The Happy Birthday Song was written in America.

    b. The Happy Birthday song has an interesting history.

    c. The Happy Birthday song is expensive to sing.

    d. How the Hill sisters became millionaires.

According to the reading:

2. The Happy Birthday song was originally about something else.   T   F

3. Mildred and Patty Hill were well-known musicians.   T   F

4. The Happy Birthday song was first written in German.   T   F

5. No one knows who changed the words to the song.   T   F

B Check your answers.

Score _____/5

C Summarize the key points in the reading. Turn to page 53.

Expansion Questions

1. What's the most popular song in the world? Do you know the words?

_____

2. Do you sing songs on special days? What songs do you sing?

_____

3. Should artists own their songs forever? When should a song become free?

_____

Harry Potter

Why have these books become so successful?

Harry Potter is a series of books written by an English woman named J.K. Rowling between 1997 and 2007. It is the bestselling book series in history. When it was first written, the first Harry Potter book was rejected by eight different book companies, and Rowling almost gave up. However, the ninth company accepted the
5   book, and it soon became a bestseller.

The books are about a young boy in England whose parents died when he was a baby. He was sent to live with his aunt and uncle, who were not kind to him. One day, Harry gets a special letter from a magic school. Soon, he finds out that he is a wizard and can do magic. At the magic school, Harry meets two
10 other students, Ron Weasley and Hermione Granger, and the three become good friends. Harry learns that a very bad wizard named Voldemort killed his parents and that now Harry and his friends must try to find and kill him.

Some parts of the story are funny. Other parts are sad. But the books are always exciting. People say that the Harry Potter books made kids want to read
15 for fun again, like they used to before movies and computer games. On the other hand, some others have said that Harry Potter is bad for children. These people don't like the mention of magic in the stories and say that such stories are not good for children.

20 Whatever you may think of Harry Potter, it is hard to argue with its success. J.K. Rowling has sold almost 500 million books, and this has made her one of the richest people in
25 the world. There are movies, video games, and countless toys based on the stories. Today, not even Voldemort could make Harry Potter go away.

Time

A Circle the right answer.

1. The main idea in this reading is:
   a. How the Harry Potter movies were made.
   b. How Harry Potter and his friends became wizards.
   c. Why J.K. Rowling is one of the top writers in the world.
   d. That Harry Potter is a very popular book series.

According to the reading:

2. J.K. Rowling sold many books before Harry Potter.   T   F
3. The first Harry Potter book was written in the 1990s.   T   F
4. J.K. Rowling gives all her Harry Potter money away.   T   F
5. Some people say that Harry Potter is bad for children.   T   F

B Check your answers.

Score _____/5

C Summarize the key points in the reading. Turn to page 53.

Expansion Questions

1. What was your favorite book or movie when you were a child?
   _____

2. Do you believe in magic? What would you do if you had magic powers?
   _____

3. Are stories about magic or ghosts OK for children to read?
   _____

Alice in Wonderland

Who wrote this popular book, and why?

Alice's Adventures in Wonderland is one of the most loved children's books of all time. It tells the story of a young girl named Alice, who stops doing her
5 school work in order to follow a rabbit down a rabbit hole. Through the hole, Alice enters an unusual world called Wonderland. In this world, she meets many talking animals and other unusual
10 people and animals.

The book's writer is Lewis Carroll. In fact, this was not his real name. His real name was Charles Dodgson. One day, Dodgson took a boat ride down the
15 Thames River in England with three little girls who were friends of the family. To keep them happy, he made up a story in which Alice, one of the children, was the main character in the story. They enjoyed the story very much.

20 Dodgson later wrote down the story and gave it to Alice as a present. He also gave the story to a friend. This friend read it to his children, and they loved it too. He suggested to Dodgson that he make a book from his story. Dodgson then wrote more parts to the story and sold it as a book. It quickly became a bestseller.

One of its first readers was Queen Victoria. She asked for a collection of all of
25 Lewis Carroll's works. She was surprised to find that there were many works on mathematics. In fact, Charles Dodgson was also a well-known mathematician. We can see this in the many puzzles that appear in his books.

Since the story first appeared, it has been sold in over fifty languages and has had several movies based on it. Today, the book *Alice's Adventures in Wonderland*
30 is often sold together with the next book about Alice, *Through the Looking Glass*.

A Circle the right answer.

1. The main idea in this reading is:

   a. How Lewis Carroll created the Alice books.

   b. How Alice traveled to Wonderland and back.

   c. Why Queen Victoria loved children's books.

   d. How George Dodgson became a mathematician.

According to the reading:

2. George Dodgson and Lewis Carroll are the same person.   T   F

3. Queen Victoria did not like the Alice books.   T   F

4. Alice was a real person.   T   F

5. George Dodgson loved puzzles.   T   F

B Check your answers.

Score _____/5

C Summarize the key points in the reading. Turn to page 53.

Expansion Questions

1. Do you know the story of *Alice in Wonderland?* What do you remember?

   _____

2. What is the best-known children's story in your country?

   _____

3. Do you know any writers? How do they get their ideas for stories?

   _____

Street Art

Is graffiti art or just vandalism?

People have been making graffiti for thousands of years. Explorers have found them in ancient Egypt, in Roman cities, and even on prehistoric cave walls. Today, we can see colorful spray-painted graffiti on the walls of almost every major city around the world. Some see graffiti as a kind of art, but many others call it
5   vandalism.

People who don't like graffiti say that it is simply vandalism. They may have a point; after all, if you paint your house, you would not like it if someone came at night and painted whatever they wanted on your wall—especially if they painted words you don't agree with, or an image you don't like. It's true that graffiti does
10 damage people's property.

On the other hand, graffiti can be artistic, funny, or have an important message. This kind of graffiti is loved by many people. The mysterious artist Banksy, for example, has become very well known for his or her graffiti. Banksy's work often carries a sharp political message; for example, "If at first you don't succeed, call an
15 airstrike." Banksy's art pieces are sometimes removed and sold for a lot of money.

People who support graffiti art say it adds beauty to a place. This is especially true in the poorer, dirtier places where graffiti is most common. In such places, graffiti can give a voice to young people. Supporters of graffiti say that we should help young artists, not try to stop them.

20 Maybe the most important thing to remember about graffiti is that it is not all the same. In some situations, graffiti can be beautiful—but in others, it is nothing more than vandalism. Just like any other art,
25 some graffiti is good, and some graffiti is bad. We should look at each piece with an open mind.

Time _____

A Circle the right answer.

1. The main idea in this reading is:

a. Graffiti is not art, but a crime like vandalism.

b. Graffiti is art and should be in a museum.

c. People disagree about what graffiti is.

d. Graffiti is made by angry young people.

According to the reading:

2.	Some people believe that graffiti is beautiful.	T	F
3.	Banksy is a brand of high-quality spray paint.	T	F
4.	Some graffiti uses political messages.	T	F
5.	Graffiti damages people's property.	T	F

B Check your answers.

Score _____/5

C Summarize the key points in the reading. Turn to page 53.

Expansion Questions

1. What is the best-known piece of art in the world? Where is it?

_____

2. Who decides if a piece of art is good or bad?

_____

3. What kind of art do you like? Do many other people also like it?

_____

SUMMARIZE ≫≫≫

Summarize the key points in the readings. Include the words in the box.
You can look back at the text when you do this.

13 The Happy Birthday Song

| lyrics | song book | teachers | protect |

_____

_____

_____

_____

14 Harry Potter

| rejected | magic school | richest | written |

_____

_____

_____

_____

15 Alice in Wonderland

| rabbit hole | mathematician | boat ride | bestseller |

_____

_____

_____

_____

16 Graffiti

| ancient | vandalism | beauty | vandalism |

_____

_____

_____

_____

5 Science and Technology

1. Would you like to take an online course? Why or why not?
2. What are the good and bad sides of living to be 200 years old?
3. How will self-driving cars change our lives?

RED SEA, SUDAN—A diver photographs an octopus hiding in the coral off the coast of Sudan.

17 Online Education

√	Keyword	Category	Definition	Use in a sentence
	education			
	distance		the space between things	
	file-sharing			
	apps			
	technology			
	face-to-face			
	video chat			
	social media	noun		
	university			
	degree			I graduated with a degree in mathematics.

18 The End of Aging

√	Keyword	Category	Definition	Use in a sentence
	medicine			The doctor gave me medicine for my cold.
	technology			
	average	noun		
	developed			
	beyond		past a certain point	
	age	verb		
	anti-	prefix		
	imagine			
	machine			
	cancer			

19 Octopus Intelligence

✓	Keyword	Category	Definition	Use in a sentence
	smartest			
	backbone			
	hide			
	tank			There are 20 liters of water in the fish tank.
	crab			
	steal		to take something without paying for it	
	trap	noun		
	aquarium			
	pipe			
	survival			

20 Self-Driving Cars

✓	Keyword	Category	Definition	Use in a sentence
	self-driving			
	accident			
	second		1/60 of a minute	
	mistakes			
	careless	adjective		
	rule	noun		
	decide			
	real-time			
	perfect			
	unexpected			If you don't plan, unexpected things can happen.

Online Education

Is learning online as good as learning in the classroom?

Online education is a kind of distance education. Online courses are offered through the internet using video, file-sharing apps, 5 email, and other technologies. This is good for students who live too far away from a school, who work full-time, who cannot move around easily, or who simply want to study 10 from home.

Distance education is not a new idea. People have been taking courses through the mail for many years. In the early forms of distance education, the teacher would mail out work for students to watch or read. Students would 15 then mail their completed work back to the teacher. It was very slow. The internet has greatly helped this. It is now much faster and easier to study by distance.

However, some people worry that online education is not as good as studying in a school with other students and teachers. These people believe that face-to-face work will always be an important part of learning. They also say that it is too 20 easy to set up an online school, so many online courses are not very good.

Supporters of online education admit that these problems may have been true in the past. However, they say, as technology has become better, so has online learning. Students and teachers today are much more comfortable using video chats and social media to talk with others and to learn from each other. 25 There are also better government rules to make sure online education is good.

Today, there are many very good online courses to choose from, and most students do at least part of their coursework online. Most universities offer some courses or whole degrees which are 100% online. In fact, there are now some completely online universities—that is, universities which do not have any 30 classrooms at all.

Time _____

Circle the right answer.

1. The main idea in this reading is:

   a. What distance education is and how it is changing.

   b. How online education is better than distance education.

   c. What kind of people are taking online education.

   d. How dangerous studying online can be.

According to the reading:

2. There was no distance education before the internet.   T   F
3. Some people think face-to-face education is better.   T   F
4. Some universities today are completely online.   T   F
5. Social media is not good for online education.   T   F

Check your answers.

   Score _____ /5

Summarize the key points in the reading. Turn to page 65.

Expansion Questions

1. Have you ever learned to make or do something online?

   _____

2. Can you think of some good and bad points about studying online?

   _____

3. What is the best way to learn something new, in person or online?

   _____

The End of Aging

Can science help us to live much longer lives?

In recent times, discoveries in medicine and technology have meant that humans now live longer than before. For example, in 1960,
5 the average person in developed countries lived to be about 70 years old. By 2010, the average had gone up to over 80 years. Today, it is not unusual for many people to reach
10 their 90th birthday and beyond.

It isn't just that we are living longer. We are living better, too. New technologies, better healthcare, information about how to live, and better eating not only make our life longer,
15 but also make it better as well. A healthy 60-year-old today is often happier and does more than a 60-year-old who lived in the early 1900s.

In fact, our life is getting better so quickly that a group of scientists now say that the next step is to end aging completely. This group, called the anti-aging movement, believes that we can use drugs and technology to make our lives far
20 longer than most people today can even imagine. One of its leaders, Ray Kurzweil, has said that soon humans will be able to live forever.

Another leader of the anti-aging movement, Aubrey de Grey, believes that most of the technology needed to slow down aging is already here. He says that the human body is like a machine; we can continue to change parts and keep it
25 working. But first, we must stop thinking of aging as something that we can't stop. Instead, he says, we should fight aging in the same way that we fight cancer.

Many scientists agree with these ideas. In fact, most scientists today think it is possible to make the average human life last around 90 years. What they don't agree on yet is how long it will take to reach this goal.

Time _____

A Circle the right answer.

1. The main idea in this reading is:
   a. It may be possible for people to live much longer lives.
   b. The anti-aging movement wants people to stay young forever.
   c. Today, the average person's life is about 90 years.
   d. Medicine and technology are changing the world.

According to the reading:

2. Ray Kurzweil died in 1960.   T   F
3. Many scientists agree that our lives can be longer.   T   F
4. Aubrey de Grey wants us to think about aging in a different way.   T   F
5. Today, 60-year-olds are happier than 60-year-olds in the 1920s.   T   F

B Check your answers.

Score _____ /5

C Summarize the key points in the reading. Turn to page 65.

Expansion Questions

1. Who is the oldest person you know? How old is he or she?
   _____

2. If you could replace your body with a new body, would you do it?
   _____

3. How would humanity change if we could live for 300 years?
   _____

Octopus Intelligence

Is the octopus really one of the smartest animals?

5 The octopus may look strange with its eight legs and small body, but it is in fact one of the smartest animals in the world. Interestingly, the octopus is an animal without a backbone. Although we know of many smart animals with backbones, such as dogs or cats, the octopus is the only animal without 10 a backbone that is so smart.

Scientists say that octopuses can learn information and then use it in new ways. For example, they sometimes climb inside fishing boats and hide in tanks full of crabs, one of 15 their favorite foods. They have also learned how to steal fish from traps.

One well-known example happened about 100 years ago at an aquarium in England. An octopus came out of its tank at night, climbed into another tank nearby, ate the fish that was in that tank, and then moved back into its own tank. This happened several times before aquarium workers discovered what was 20 happening. In another well-known story, Inky, an octopus in New Zealand, got out of his tank, went down a pipe, and found his way back to the sea.

Octopuses are also able to play. In one study, scientists wanted to know if two octopuses would play together the same way that dogs or cats do. They put an empty bottle into an octopus tank, and soon the two octopuses were shooting 25 water at the bottle. They pushed the bottle backwards and forwards between them just like kids playing with a ball. This shows that octopuses can use the things around them for reasons other than survival.

These stories may not seem like much when we see what we humans can do. For animals, however, they put the octopus at about the same level as many others 30 we think of as very smart.

Time

A Circle the right answer.

1. The main idea in this reading is:
   a. How octopuses are very playful animals.
   b. How octopuses often escape from tanks.
   c. How octopuses are surprisingly smart animals.
   d. Why we shouldn't eat octopuses.

According to the reading:

2. There are many smart animals with no backbone.   T   F
3. Octopuses like to eat crabs and fish.   T   F
4. Inky was a famous dog who loved octopuses.   T   F
5. Octopuses like to play.   T   F

B Check your answers.

Score _____/5

C Summarize the key points in the reading. Turn to page 65.

Expansion Questions

1. What is the most intelligent animal on earth, after humans?

   _____

2. Do you think we should give intelligent animals special rights?

   _____

3. Would an octopus make a good pet? Why or why not?

   _____

Self-Driving Cars

Can computers drive better than people can?

Driving is dangerous. Every year, in almost every country in the world, people die in car accidents. In 2013, more than one million people worldwide died because of car accidents. That means one person every 25 seconds, or six or seven deaths by the time you finish reading this page. How can we find an answer to
5   this problem? Many people think that the answer will be computer-controlled self-driving cars.

In the United States, 81% of road deaths are caused by humans making mistakes. Self-driving cars, however, don't make mistakes. They are not careless, they don't get tired, and they never need to stop. They always follow the rules
10   of the road, and they decide what to do thousands of times faster than even the best human driver. These computer-controlled cars can talk to the internet and talk with other cars around them in real-time, so they always know where they are and how long it will take to get to where they're going.

However, self-driving cars are not perfect—not yet. For example, tests show
15   that the cars sometimes have trouble when driving at night or in bad weather. Also, although computers don't make mistakes, they cannot think either. Human drivers, when faced with an unexpected situation, can usually think of something to do. A computer, on the other hand, may not be able to decide what to do and may do nothing.

20   Self-driving technology is getting better and better every day. The question is no longer *if* self-driving cars will take over, but *when*. People now believe
25   that in a few more years most cars on the road will be self-driving. Soon after that, all cars will be self-driving. At that point, driving will become something to
30   be enjoyed only on special roads, like horse riding is today.

(Time) _____

A Circle the right answer.

1. The main idea in this reading is:
   a. The good and bad points of self-driving cars.
   b. How the self-driving car was invented.
   c. Why human drivers kill so many people each year.
   d. How self-driving cars will destroy driving jobs.

According to the reading:

2. Self-driving cars don't make mistakes.   T   F
3. Self-driving cars will be controlled by the internet.   T   F
4. Human drivers are better in unexpected situations.   T   F
5. One day, driving a car will be a hobby like horse riding. T   F

B Check your answers.

Score _____/5

C Summarize the key points in the reading. Turn to page 65.

Expansion Questions

1. Can you drive a car? Are you a good driver?

   _____

2. What are the good and bad points about self-driving cars?

   _____

3. If you had a self-driving car, how would your life change?

   _____

SUMMARIZE ≫≫≫

Summarize the key points in the readings. Include the words in the box. You can look back at the text when you do this.

17 Online Education

internet	face-to-face	mail	universities

_____

_____

_____

_____

18 The End of Aging

longer	better	movement	change parts

_____

_____

_____

_____

19 Octopus Intelligence

backbone	learn	play	stories

_____

_____

_____

_____

20 Self-Driving Cars

dangerous	mistakes	decide	computers

_____

_____

_____

_____

6 Business

1. Do you think all countries could use one money system? Think of the good and bad points.
2. What are some of the most successful video game companies? What do you know about them?

21 One World Currency

✓	Keyword	Category	Definition	Use in a sentence
	include			
	currency			The euro is the official currency of Ireland.
	value	noun		
	cows			
	compare			
	online			
	goods			
	nationalism		a strong belief in the greatness of your country	
	European Union			
	euro			

22 Nintendo

✓	Keyword	Category	Definition	Use in a sentence
	video games			
	market		a place where goods are sold and bought	
	huge			
	billion			
	entertainment			
	business			
	series			
	cute			
	prime minister	noun		
	Olympics			The original Olympics were held in Greece.

23 The Business of Sport

✓	Keyword	Category	Definition	Use in a sentence
	church			
	Manchester			
	fighting			
	busy		having many things to do and no free time	
	soccer			
	stadium			
	uniform			At my high school, boys wore blue uniforms.
	advertise	verb		
	connected			
	medal			

24 The Tulip Bubble

✓	Keyword	Category	Definition	Use in a sentence
	supply		noun	
	demand	noun		
	reasonable			
	bubble			
	pop			The balloon popped with a loud sound.
	drop	verb		
	Holland			
	tulip			
	borrow			
	uncertainty		not sure; not knowing what may happen	

One World Currency

Would it be better if all countries used the same currency?

The history of money started when people needed to pay for things that they wanted. Early forms of money included animals, food, and valuable stones. Today we use paper money, or currency. Currency has no value by itself like cows or food do, but it shows value. Each country protects the value of their own currency—for
5 example, the peso in Mexico, the won in Korea, the lira in Turkey, the dollar in Canada, and so on.

However, the value of one currency is always going up or down compared to the other currencies. This can cause difficulty for business
10 between countries and for people who travel a lot. For this reason, people sometimes suggest that the whole world should use just one single
15 currency. This world currency would have the same value whether you are in Japan, Mexico, Korea, Turkey, or any other country.

20 There are some clear good points to a single world currency. First, people would not need to use different money when they travel. Also, it would be easy to understand the price of things in other countries or when shopping online. It could also make selling goods between countries easier and
25 help smaller countries.

On the other hand, there are some problems. Perhaps the biggest is that countries would not be able to change the value of their own currency, which they sometimes do now. Another problem might be feelings of nationalism. People in many countries today like their own currency and do not want to change it.

30 Actually, we already have one good example of what could happen if we changed to a single world currency. Before the European Union, each European country had their own currency. Today, most have changed to the euro, while some, like Sweden and Switzerland, continue to use their own currencies.

Time

A Circle the right answer.

1. The main idea in this reading is:

a. The best kind of currency is paper money.

b. Every country should have its own currency.

c. Currency values are always going up and down.

d. A single world currency has good and bad points.

According to the reading:

2. Cows used to be used as a kind of money.	T	F
3. Many countries want to control the value of their currency.	T	F
4. A single world currency would be bad for travelers.	T	F
5. The euro is used in Sweden and Switzerland.	T	F

B Check your answers.

Score _____/5

C Summarize the key points in the reading. Turn to page 77.

Expansion Questions

1. How many currencies can you name? Which one is used in your country?

_____

2. What is the most valuable currency in the world? Where is it from?

_____

3. If money suddenly lost all value, what could you use as currency?

_____

Nintendo

What made this company a leader in video games?

In the early 1980s, video games were everywhere. The video game market was huge as game centers came into the home. The largest company at the time was Atari, controlling most of this three-billion-dollar business. In 1983, however, the video game business went through very hard times, and two years later it had lost
5 97% of its value. Many video game companies closed, but one carried on. It went on to bring the video game business back to life, almost by itself. That company was Nintendo.

Nintendo introduced the Nintendo Entertainment System, known as "NES" or "Famicon," in 1985, and soon the company was making a lot of money again. The
10 reason for this was games. Before this time, anyone could make computer games, so many of the games were not well made and not much fun. Nintendo, however, closely controlled who could make their games. This way they could make sure that the games were very good.

Since 1985, Nintendo has continued to
15 be one of the most important companies in the video game business. In that time, they have sold many game systems and games. One reason they continued to do well is that they have changed again
20 and again, always trying to find what users want. Their best game systems, like the Game Boy and the Wii, have brought something new to gaming. Nintendo has also made some of

25 the best-known games in the world. The best known is the Mario series of games. That cute little man and his friends have become so well known that when the Japanese prime minister went on stage at the closing of the 2016 Olympics, he dressed as Mario to ask everyone to come to Tokyo in 2020. Perhaps this shows that Nintendo really has become the biggest name in games.

Time _____

A Circle the right answer.

1. The main idea in this reading is:
   a. Some of the best video games were created in the 1980s.
   b. Atari and other companies competed against Nintendo.
   c. Nintendo was and still is an important video game company.
   d. Video games are an important part of Japanese culture.

According to the reading:

2. Nintendo made the NES in the 1980s.   T   F
3. Nintendo closely controlled the quality of their games.   T   F
4. The prime minister of Japan dressed up as Mario.   T   F
5. Nintendo worked with Sony to create the PlayStation.   T   F

B Check your answers.

Score _____/5

C Summarize the key points in the reading. Turn to page 77.

Expansion Questions

1. Do you play video games? What is your favorite game?
   _____

2. How many video game companies can you name? Which is the biggest?
   _____

3. What are the best-known video game characters in your country?
   _____

The Business of Sport

Is it OK that there is so much money involved in sports?

In 1880, members of St. Mark's Church in the city of Manchester, UK, were worried about problems in their city. Young men who couldn't
5 find work were drinking too much and fighting with each other. The answer, they decided, was to keep these young men busy by playing a sport, so they started a soccer
10 club. Over time, this club grew and changed to become one of the best soccer clubs in the world, Manchester City.

It has been a long time since
15 sport was just something to keep young men healthy and out of trouble. Sport is now a billion-dollar business, where making money is often more important than winning. Now, companies pay large amounts of money to put their names in the stadiums where teams play. Other companies also pay to have their names put on the team uniforms, and players can make more money in one week than most
20 people make in ten years.

It's not only soccer. Money now rules all major sports. For example, the Olympics has businesses that pay to advertise their goods during the games. This sometimes means that the Olympics becomes connected with places that sell cheap, unhealthy food. It also means that sports players are not only trying to win
25 a gold medal. They are trying to win real gold too.

To be fair, money in sport has also helped sport. Players now are much better than they used to be. They are paid enough money to train full-time and harder and longer than before. This has made for better and more exciting games. The problem with this is that it has also made sport a serious business.
30 Perhaps it would be better if all this money was taken away, and then everyone could go back to just playing for fun.

Time _____

A Circle the right answer.

1. The main idea in this reading is:
   a. How money has changed sports.
   b. How sports stars make their money.
   c. How sponsors control sports events.
   d. How too much money has made soccer less fun.

According to the reading:

2. Manchester City has a well-known Olympics team.   T   F
3. Companies sometimes pay players to lose games.   T   F
4. The Olympics was started to keep young men from fighting.   T   F
5. Today, players can train full-time, so games are more exciting.   T   F

B Check your answers.

Score _____/5

C Summarize the key points in the reading. Turn to page 77.

Expansion Questions

1. Do you know any high-level sports players? Are they professional players?

   _____

2. What are the good and bad points of money in sports?

   _____

3. Is it OK for companies to put their names on uniforms and stadiums?

   _____

The Tulip Bubble

What is a bubble economy?

Supply and demand are the main reasons why the price of something goes up or down. When there is high demand but low supply, prices go up; when there is low demand but high supply, prices go down.

With most goods, prices stay at a reasonable level—not too high, not too
5   low. Sometimes, however, when there is very high demand and supply can't catch up, prices can rise out of control. This is called a bubble.

Bubbles are dangerous because they can "pop" at any time, causing prices to drop. One of the earliest bubbles happened in Holland over flowers. It shows that bubbles can happen for almost
10 anything.

In the 1630s, people were very excited about tulips in Holland. They had recently been brought to Europe, so they were new and exciting.
15 Demand for the flowers went up quickly, and people saw a chance to make money. Many of them borrowed money to buy tulips, then sold them the next day for a higher
20 price. They could pay back what they borrowed and keep the extra money. It seemed like a good plan.

From 1634 to 1637, the plan worked well. The price of tulips went up and up. By February 1637, one tulip cost ten times more than a worker made in one
25 year. Many people became very rich. However, the situation could not continue.

One day, no one bought any tulips. This caused uncertainty, and the price of tulips suddenly dropped. Many people lost all their money. Some lost their homes. Reality had returned to the tulip market.

Since Holland's tulip bubble, there have been many others. Perhaps the
30 best-known recent bubble was the "dot-com" bubble of 1997-2001, when even the largest technology companies lost up to 80% of their value within a few months.

Time _____

A Circle the right answer.

1. The main idea in this reading is:

    a. Why people in Holland love flowers.

    b. The good and bad points about tulips.

    c. How economic bubbles can happen.

    d. How to make money during a bubble.

According to the reading:

2.	The tulip bubble started and ended within three weeks.	T	F
3.	The name 'bubble' is used because flowers grow quickly.	T	F
4.	During the bubble, one tulip cost about the same as a horse.	T	F
5.	The 'dot-com' bubble was stopped before anyone lost money.	T	F

B Check your answers.

Score _____/5

C Summarize the key points in the reading. Turn to page 77.

Expansion Questions

1. Some items become popular very quickly, then suddenly stop. Can you think of any recent examples?

_____

2. Have you ever paid more than the usual price for something that you really wanted?

_____

3. Economic bubbles can be dangerous. Should the government stop them before they get too big?

_____

SUMMARIZE

Summarize the key points in the readings. Include the words in the box. You can look back at the text when you do this.

21 One World Currency

currency	business	travel	problems

_____

_____

_____

_____

22 Nintendo

video games	hard times	controlled	changed

_____

_____

_____

_____

23 The Business of Sport

billion-dollar	companies	young men	advertise

_____

_____

_____

_____

24 The Tulip Bubble

supply and demand	control	value	dropped

_____

_____

_____

_____

7 Health and Medicine

1. What is your favorite way of getting exercise? Why do you like it?
2. What do you usually do when you get a cold? Does it work?
3. Why do you think some kinds of medicine are so expensive?

25 Walking for Exercise

√	Keyword	Category	Definition	Use in a sentence
	lift	verb		
	weight			
	join			
	studies	noun		
	fat	noun		
	percent			Only ten percent of students study every night.
	climb			
	stairs			
	necessarily			
	gym		a place where people exercise or play sports	

26 Catching a Cold

√	Keyword	Category	Definition	Use in a sentence
	cold	noun		
	widespread	adjective		
	illness			
	spread			
	cough			I need some medicine to cure my cough.
	virus			
	handle	noun		
	medicine			
	headache			
	runny nose		when water comes out of your nose	

27 Herbal Medicines

✓	Keyword	Category	Definition	Use in a sentence
	herbs			
	diseases			
	throughout	prep.		
	medicine			
	allowed		being permitted to do something; given permission	
	garlic			
	ginseng			
	ginger	noun		
	blood pressure			My doctor says that my blood pressure is too high.
	stomach			

28 Generic Medicine

✓	Keyword	Category	Definition	Use in a sentence
	medicine			
	drug			
	generic	adjective		
	expensive			
	cost	noun		
	disease			
	waste			Don't waste your money on this item; it's not good.
	right away		immediately; now	
	available			
	trust			

Walking for Exercise

Is walking as good for health as other forms of exercise?

People exercise in different ways. Some lift weights or join a dance class. Others ride bicycles or play a team sport. However, one of the best ways to exercise is also the simplest: walking. Studies show that walking helps to lose weight, makes the heart stronger, and makes you less likely to become ill. It is also
5   easy to do since most of us already do it every day.

Perhaps the best thing about walking is that it burns fat without making your body work too hard. Running or playing sports also burn fat, but you have a higher chance of hurting yourself. For example, running and jumping sports can cause trouble for your legs.

10   Another good thing about walking is that it makes your heart stronger. With a strong heart, you are less likely to have heart trouble. One study shows that walking for thirty minutes a day can make you thirty percent less likely to have heart trouble.

Doctors suggest any amount of walking for your health. However, the best is to
15   walk for thirty minutes a day, every day. You should be able to walk comfortably. If it feels too easy, walk faster; if you get out of breath, slow down.

Walking does not have to feel like work. Make it fun. Take your dog with you, or ask a friend to come along. Some people get all the walking they need simply by climbing the stairs at work or school. At night, take a walk instead of using the
20   computer.

The main point is that it is not necessary to join a gym or spend money to be healthy. Any exercise is good for you,
25   and walking is already something that most people do every day. Why not make it a bigger part of your life?

A Circle the right answer.

1. The main idea in this reading is:
   a. There are good and bad points about walking.
   b. Walking is better than running or riding a bicycle.
   c. Many people are in danger of having heart trouble.
   d. Walking is a good way to exercise, and anyone can do it.

According to the reading:

2. Doctors say that only walking short distances is not good.   T   F
3. Walking regularly can help us avoid illness.   T   F
4. The best amount of walking is thirty minutes every day.   T   F
5. We can try to make walking fun by doing it with a friend.   T   F

B Check your answers.

Score _____/5

C Summarize the key points in the reading. Turn to page 89.

Expansion Questions

1. How far do you walk each day? Do you enjoy walking?
   _____

2. How could you change your life so that you can walk more?
   _____

3. What other daily activities are good exercise?
   _____

Catching a Cold

How can we avoid catching colds?

Colds are the most widespread illness on earth. Almost everyone will catch a cold during their life. People
5 like teachers and doctors sometimes catch several colds in one year. A cold can last from one to two weeks and is the main cause of visits
10 to the doctor and missed days from school and work.

Some people do not understand how we catch colds. It is not true that you
15 can catch a cold from cold weather. Most people catch colds during the fall and winter, but this is not because the weather is colder; it is because people spend more time at home near each other.

Colds spread mostly from touching. You can also get sick by touching anything a sick person has touched, such as a phone or door. On the other hand, when
20 people cough, it is not as easy to catch their cold. This is because the virus does not live very long in the air. It must live on something like books, door handles or a computer keyboard. Keeping your hands clean is an important way to stop getting a cold. When you come into your house after shopping, for example, wash your hands.

25 Another reason that winter is the time for colds is because there is less water in the air, which helps cold viruses to live longer. Dry air also makes the inside of our noses drier, which is helpful for the virus.

Although there is nothing to kill a cold, you can help your body to get better. First, take medicine for headaches and coughing. Second, drink lots of water;
30 coughing and a runny nose happen when your body tries to push out the virus. Most importantly, rest; your body needs to be at full strength to help it fight the virus.

Time _____

A Circle the right answer.

1. The main idea in this reading is:

   a. How to stop a cold once it has started.

   b. What a cold is and how we catch it.

   c. The three best ways to avoid catching a cold.

   d. The good and bad points about cold medicines.

According to the reading:

2. We can catch a cold from sleeping in a cold room.	T	F
3. The cold virus loves warm, wet air.	T	F
4. It is easier to catch a cold from a cough than by touch.	T	F
5. You can kill the cold virus by drinking strong medicine.	T	F

B Check your answers.

Score _____ /5

C Summarize the key points in the reading. Turn to page 89.

Expansion Questions

1. When was the last time you had a cold? How did you feel?

_____

2. How and where do people usually catch colds?

_____

3. If you catch a cold, what can you do to feel better?

_____

Herbal Medicine

Is herbal medicine effective? Is it safe?

Plants which are used for health and well-being are often called herbs. Thousands of years ago, people used herbs to fight diseases and stay healthy. In North America alone, people used more than 3,000 different herbs. Today, people throughout the world still use herbs for health reasons. In fact, many of the medicines
5 we use today came from herbs.

Usually, when people talk about herbal medicine, they mean medicine which is not made or tested by science. For this reason, in many countries, doctors are not allowed to give herbal medicines to sick people. However, most people around the world have tried some kind of herbal medicine at least once. In fact,
10 many of these herbs are sold in supermarkets and used as food.

Garlic, for example, is often used in cooking. It is said to fight heart disease and the cold. Ginseng
15 is another well-known herb. It is said to be good for blood pressure and help the body fight disease. Another plant, ginger, may help if you have stomach trouble. Some
20 flowers are also used as herbal medicines. Herbal medicine is often used to make you sleep better, to help you feel less worried, and to fight disease.

Today, it is easy to buy herbal medicines from around the world using the
25 internet. For this reason, it is important to remember that some herbs are powerful and can damage the human body. Also, some herbs which you can buy in one country may not be allowed in another, which could get you in trouble with the police.

Herbal medicines have been around for thousands of years and will continue to
30 be used by many people. However, we should always be careful when choosing what to put into our bodies. Sometimes, the medicine can be worse than the disease.

Time _____

A Circle the right answer.

1. The main idea in this reading is:
   a. Herbal medicines are popular all around the world.
   b. Herbal medicines can be dangerous for children.
   c. Herbal medicines were popular 3,000 years ago.
   d. Doctors are not allowed to give out herbal medicines.

According to the reading:

2. Herbal medicines can include plants and animal bones.   T   F
3. Herbal medicines are usually tested by science.   T   F
4. Herbal medicines can be dangerous for your body.   T   F
5. These days, most people try to avoid herbal medicines.   T   F

B Check your answers.

Score _____/5

C Summarize the key points in the reading. Turn to page 89.

Expansion Questions

1. When you feel sick, do you usually take medicine?

   _____

2. What kind of medicine is best, natural medicine or medicine made in a laboratory?

   _____

3. Do you know any plants that are good medicine? What are they?

   _____

Generic Medicine

What is it, and why is it cheaper than other medicine?

Doctors often tell people to take medicines which are made by large drug companies. However, sometimes there is also a generic
5　medicine which does the same job. The generic medicine is the same but is made by a less well-known company.

Some people want to use
10　these generic medicines because they are usually less expensive. Because generic medicines are made in the same way, they should do the same job as the better-known medicines. So why pay more?

15　Generic medicines are cheaper than other medicines because they do not include the costs of discovering the medicine. To make a new medicine, drug companies must first pay scientists to study a disease and to suggest a new medicine to fight it. Then, they must spend money testing the new medicine to make sure that it is safe and that it works. If these tests do not work, the money is wasted.
20　That is why, once a company does find a good medicine, they will set a high price for it. They are trying to get back not only the money that they spent on this medicine, but also some of the money they spent on all their testing.

Generic medicine makers, on the other hand, simply use medicines that have already been discovered and tested. For this reason, they do not spend as much
25　money to make medicines. This is why generic medicines are usually not sold right away; the companies that want to make them must wait a number of years before they can make the same medicine.

When the generic medicine is available to buy, doctors are usually quick to tell people about it. Taking generic medicines can save people a lot of money.
30　Still, some people like the well-known medicines because they feel that they can trust them more.

Time

A Circle the right answer.

1. The main idea in this reading is:
   a. Why doctors don't like to give out generic medicines.
   b. Why generic medicines are better than well-known medicines.
   c. What generic medicines are and how they are made.
   d. How companies try to copy each other's medicines.

According to the reading:

2. Generic medicines are often stronger and last longer.   T   F
3. Well-known medicines are more expensive than generics.   T   F
4. It is a waste of money to make generic medicines.   T   F
5. Doctors are quick to tell people about generic medicines.   T   F

B Check your answers.

Score _____/5

C Summarize the key points in the reading. Turn to page 89.

Expansion Questions

1. Have you been to a doctor recently? Did he or she give you medicine?
   _____

2. Why do you think some medicines are so expensive?
   _____

3. Should a company be able to copy another company's medicine and make it cheaper?
   _____

Summarize the key points in the readings. Include the words in the box. You can look back at the text when you do this.

25 Walking for Exercise

fun	fat	heart	thirty

_____

_____

_____

_____

26 Catching a Cold

cold weather	widespread	touching	dry air

_____

_____

_____

_____

27 Herbal Medicines

science	garlic	ginseng	careful

_____

_____

_____

_____

28 Generic Medicine

less expensive	discovering	testing	drug companies

_____

_____

_____

_____

8 The Universe

1. Who was the first person in outer space? Who was the first person on the Moon?
2. Would you like to live on another planet? Why or why not?
3. What do you know about the Big Bang?

INTERNATIONAL SPACE STATION—A view of our planet from outer

29 The Space Race

✓	Keyword	Category	Definition	Use in a sentence
	Soviet Union			The Soviet Union included Russia and many other countries.
	satellite			
	World War II			
	cold war		a war without physical fighting	
	president			
	the Moon	proper noun		
	statement			
	land	verb		
	leap		a long jump	
	mankind			

30 Moons for Living On

✓	Keyword	Category	Definition	Use in a sentence
	disaster			So many people died in the disaster.
	dinosaurs			
	humanity			
	planet			
	Venus		the second planet from the Sun	
	Jupiter			
	Saturn			
	Titan	proper noun		
	oxygen			
	materials			

31 Are We Aliens?

✓	Keyword	Category	Definition	Use in a sentence
	planet			
	alien			a living thing from another planet
	professor			
	university			
	RNA	noun (acronym)		
	suitable			
	unlike			
	probably			I'll probably go, but I'm not 100% sure yet.
	virus			
	lifeform			

32 The Big Bang

✓	Keyword	Category	Definition	Use in a sentence
	deeply			
	religion			
	bang		a sudden, loud explosion	
	universe			
	packed			
	tightly			
	matter	noun		
	energy			Solar energy is used in more and more homes.
	blow up			
	bomb	noun		

The Space Race

Which country really won the space race?

After World War II, the two most powerful countries in the world were the United States and the Soviet Union. Although
5 they had worked together during WWII, now they were not friends. In fact, they started fighting a "cold war" when WWII ended. One of the ways they fought
10 with each other was through technology; both countries wanted to show that they were the most powerful and had the best technology.

15 The space race was started by the Soviet Union in 1957 when
it sent up the satellite Sputnik 1. It was the first time that humans put a satellite around the Earth. This surprised the United States. Four years later, the Soviets did it again when they sent the first person into space. That man, Yuri Gagarin, became a
20 hero in the Soviet Union.

The United States could not believe it. They needed to do something bigger and better. President Kennedy, in 1962, promised that the United States would put a man on the Moon by 1969. It was a brave statement, and many people did not believe it was possible.

25 However, on July 20th, 969, Apollo 11 safely landed on the Moon. Neil Armstrong became the first person to walk on the Moon, with the well-known words, "That's one small step for [a] man, a giant leap for mankind." It was what the United States needed. They had won this part of the space race.

In the end, the Soviet Union never sent a person to the Moon, so the space
30 race ended with the Americans winning. However, both countries have continued to travel into space since then. Today, many countries—and even companies—are going into space. Most people believe that a new space race has already started: who will be the first to reach Mars?

Time

A Circle the right answer.

1. The main idea in this reading is:
   a. How and why the space race happened.
   b. The good and bad points of having a space race.
   c. Why the space race cost so much money.
   d. The difficulty of landing a person on the Moon.

According to the reading:

2. The first person in space was an American.   T   F
3. President Kennedy said, "That's a small step for man."   T   F
4. Yuri Gagarin also went to the Moon after the Americans.   T   F
5. Today there is a new space race to go back to the Moon.   T   F

B Check your answers.

Score _____/5

C Summarize the key points in the reading. Turn to page 101.

Expansion Questions

1. Have you ever watched a spaceship taking off? How was it?

_____

2. Why did people first go into space or to the Moon?

_____

3. If you could go to the Moon, would you go? Why or why not?

_____

Moons for Living On

Where else could we live in our solar system?

We have learned a lot about life on Earth. We know that terrible disasters often happen, and when they do, they can cause lots of deaths. We now know that such a disaster killed the dinosaurs and that there were many others.

So, some people worry about whether humans can continue to live on Earth.
5 They want humanity to be able to live on other planets. That way, if something serious happened on Earth, we would be able to live somewhere else. To do that, we would need to build homes on other planets, but where?

The Moon and the planets Mars and Venus are the nearest to Earth, but they are not very good for human life. Although we will surely visit Mars and the
10 Moon again, it may be difficult to build a place to live there. To do that, we would need a place where we can make air and water, grow food, and find different kinds of materials for making things.

Recently, scientists have discovered that some of the large moons around Jupiter and Saturn may be good places for humans to live. Saturn's moon Titan,
15 for example, has a lot of oxygen and is made of rock and ice, just like Earth. Although it is very cold (about -180° C), it also has many useful materials.

Jupiter's moons both have a lot of oxygen and water under ice. While they are far from the sun, they both have a hot center; this keeps the water inside from becoming ice and could be
20 used for power.

These moons are far from Earth, so they are not easy to reach. Even if we did get there, we cannot be sure that we could live there.
25 Still, perhaps we should try—our children may thank us for it!

Time _____

A Circle the right answer.

1. The main idea in this reading is:
   a. The Earth's moon is very different from other moons.
   b. It may be possible to live on moons around other planets.
   c. We will soon be visiting Mars and other planets to live there.
   d. The best place for humans to live is right here on Earth.

According to the reading:

2. Mars and Venus are good places for human to live.   T   F
3. Earth's moon is sometimes called Titan.   T   F
4. Jupiter's and Saturn's moons have water and oxygen.   T   F
5. Jupiter's and Saturn's moons are warm because of the Sun.   T   F

B Check your answers.

Score _____ /5

C Summarize the key points in the reading. Turn to page 101.

Expansion Questions

1. What are the most important things humans need to live?

   _____

2. If humans had to choose a new planet to live on, where should we go?

   _____

3. If you were going to a new planet, what would you take with you?

   _____

Are We Aliens?

Could life have come to Earth from outer space?

Over the past hundred years, books, movies, and games have told us stories about people from other planets. In many of these stories, the aliens come to Earth from the planet Mars. It is an interesting idea, but perhaps even more interesting is the fact that life from Mars may be real—and it may already be here
5   on Earth!

Professor Steven Benner at Harvard University is one person who thinks this may be true. Benner has suggested that all life on Earth, including humans, could have come from Mars. He thinks life on Earth came from RNA, an important part of life. However, the young Earth was not a suitable place for RNA to grow, unlike
10 young Mars. So, Benner suggested that maybe, billions of years ago, RNA formed on Mars and was carried to Earth on rocks.

Today we know a great deal about Mars. For example, we know that it used to have air and water and that it has many things necessary for life. We have not found life there, but if there was life on Mars, it was probably very small and
15 very simple, like viruses. If these very small lifeforms took a ride on rocks from Mars, they could then have grown and changed here on Earth, becoming all the living things around us.

We have found many rocks from Mars on Earth. They are rocks which break off and fly into space when Mars is hit by another large body. Imagine shooting
20 into a rock wall. Small pieces would break and fly off. They may fly far away. Some of these rocks from Mars flew all the way to Earth.

25 If Benner's idea is true, billions of years ago these rocks from Mars may have carried the first life to Earth.

Time _____

A Circle the right answer.

1. The main idea in this reading is:
    a. Life on Mars may have come from Earth.
    b. Stories about aliens coming to Earth may be true.
    c. There are good and bad points about life on Earth.
    d. Life on Earth may have started on Mars.

According to the reading:

2. Rocks from Mars are sometimes found on Earth.   T   F
3. When Mars was younger, it was full of life.   T   F
4. When Earth was young, it may not have been good for life. T   F
5. Professor Benner believes that there is life on Mars now. T   F

B Check your answers.

Score _____/5

C Summarize the key points in the reading. Turn to page 101.

Expansion Questions

1. Do you think there is life on other planets?

_____

2. What do you know about Mars? Is there water and air there? Is it hot or cold?

_____

3. Have you watched many movies about aliens? What's your favorite alien?

_____

The Big Bang

How did the universe start?

Where do we come from? This is a question that humans have thought about deeply for as long as we have been living.
5 Many people think that the answer can be found in religion; that is, that the Earth and all life on it were made by a god. Scientists have a different idea;
10 they believe that it all began with a bang—the Big Bang.

In the 1920s, many scientists were looking at the stars, but only two of them would shape
15 all thinking about where the universe came from. One of them was Georges Lemaitre, a Belgian. Lemaitre suggested that the universe is growing bigger and bigger and that everything is moving away from everything else.

Lemaitre said that at the beginning of the universe, everything must have been very small and packed tightly together. All matter and energy were packed
20 into a very small point, which then blew up like a great bomb. This big bang sent everything in the universe shooting away from everything else very quickly.

At the same time, in the United States, another scientist, Edwin Hubble, was also making some important discoveries. Hubble showed that, in fact, stars far away from Earth were moving away from each other at the same rate. This
25 discovery helped other scientists to look more closely at Lemaitre's ideas, and together, both men—Hubble and Lemaitre—became very well known among scientists.

The two men helped change science in the 1900s. Today, there is a lot of scientific information which supports the Big Bang. This does not mean we
30 understand it well. While we do not yet understand all of the things we need to know—for example, what caused it, or what was there before it—we do know that that the universe started with a bang.

Time _____

A Circle the right answer.

1. The main idea in this reading is:
   a. Why the Big Bang must be true.
   b. What scientists don't yet know about the Big Bang.
   c. How the Big Bang was discovered in the 1900s.
   d. The good and bad points of our universe.

According to the reading:

2. Lemaitre noticed that the universe was getting smaller.   T   F
3. The Big Bang happened when a very big star blew up.   T   F
4. Scientists today understand everything about the Big Bang.   T   F
5. Most scientists today agree that there was a Big Bang.   T   F

B Check your answers.

Score _____/5

C Summarize the key points in the reading. Turn to page 101.

Expansion Questions

1. What do you know about the origin of the universe?
   _____

2. Can you name any scientists who study space? Why are they well known?
   _____

3. If you traveled to the beginning of time, what do you think you would see?
   _____

Summarize the key points in the readings. Include the words in the box. You can look back at the text when you do this.

29 The Space Race

| Soviet Union | the Moon | cold war | Neil Armstrong |

_____

_____

_____

_____

30 Moons for Living On

| disasters | moons | planets | oxygen |

_____

_____

_____

_____

31 Are We Aliens?

| Mars | professor | RNA | lifeforms |

_____

_____

_____

_____

32 The Big Bang

| Lemaitre | packed | growing | Hubble |

_____

_____

_____

_____

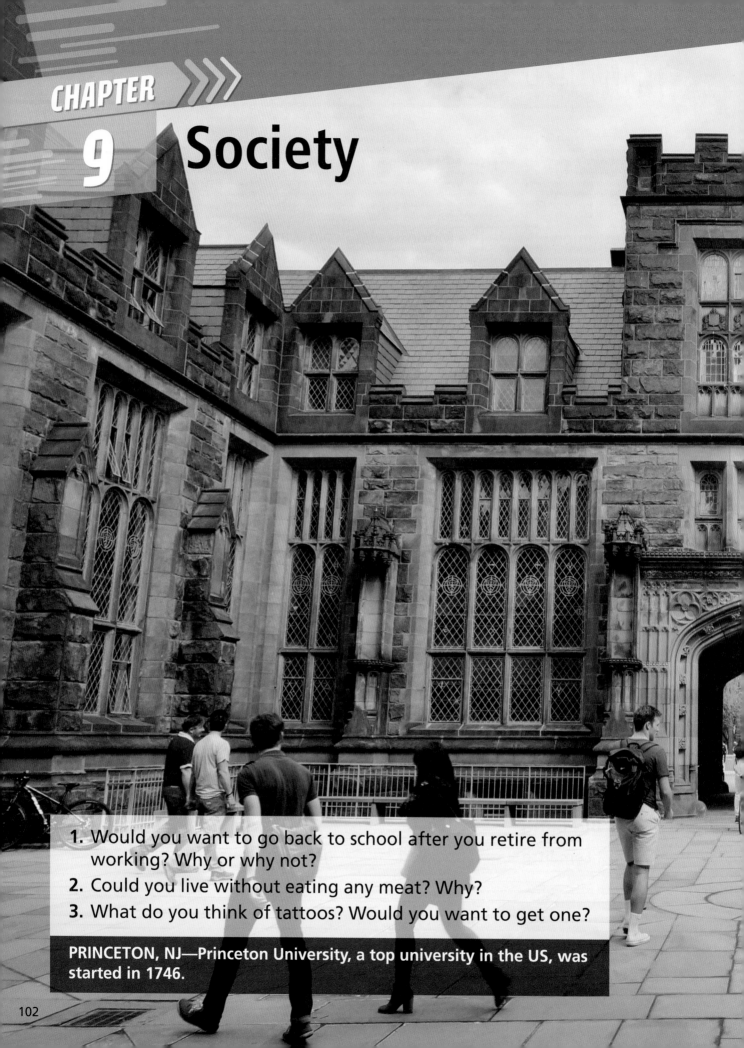

CHAPTER 9

Society

1. Would you want to go back to school after you retire from working? Why or why not?
2. Could you live without eating any meat? Why?
3. What do you think of tattoos? Would you want to get one?

PRINCETON, NJ—Princeton University, a top university in the US, was started in 1746.

33 Lifelong Learning

√	Keyword	Category	Definition	Use in a sentence
	saying	noun		
	degree			
	lifelong		all your life; from birth until death	
	expected			I'm expected to speak only in English in this class.
	illness			
	include	verb		
	language			
	training			
	related			
	interest			

34 Extreme Body Modification

√	Keyword	Category	Definition	Use in a sentence
	extreme			
	modification			
	cut out	verb		
	cosmetic	adjective		
	surgery			The man had surgery on his heart.
	models			
	stand out			
	tattoos		ink pictures drawn on the skin	
	tongue			
	lizard			

35 Vegetarianism

✓	Keyword	Category	Definition	Use in a sentence
	recent		adjective	
	figures	noun		
	vegetarian			My sister is vegetarian, but she eats fish.
	meat			
	vegan			
	common		done by many people; easily available; not special	
	Hindu	proper noun		
	percent			
	cancer			
	lifestyle			

36 How Children Learn

✓	Keyword	Category	Definition	Use in a sentence
	born			
	computer			
	store	verb		
	language			
	enough	adjective		
	pointing			
	recognize			My teacher didn't recognize me after ten years.
	college			
	pay attention		to watch something closely	
	machine			

Lifelong Learning

Can we continue our education throughout our lives?

In the United States, there is a well-known saying: "You are never too old to learn." Ocie King and Gustava Burris are perfect examples. King
5 completed her university degree at age 94; Burris got her high school degree at 97. These two women are part of a growing number of lifelong learners in the US.

Lifelong learners are people who
10 keep on studying long after they have finished the expected number of school years. Some, like Burris, had to leave school early so they could get money to help their families. Others, like King, had
15 to stop because of an illness. Other people did not have enough money or had to fight in a war.

Lifelong learning is also known as continuing education. It includes everyone
20 from people who want to learn a new language to those who want to complete a university degree. Lifelong learners may

also be taking training courses to do better in their jobs. In 2014, more than 1.5 million Americans were taking some kind of continuing education course, and
25 that number continues to grow every year.

Most lifelong learners take courses related to their work. They want to learn something new that will help them get a better job. Other courses are those related to fun such as music or art. In recent years, school degree programs, like the ones King and Burris took, have also had more older students.

30 Lifelong learning is expected to grow even more around the world. As people live longer lives, as online learning becomes easier, and as technologies such as self-driving cars take over jobs, more and more people may choose to return to school. Although many will want to learn a new job, many others, like King and Burris, may do it for the interest and the love of learning.

Time

A Circle the right answer.

1. The main idea in this reading is:

    a. The good and bad points of lifelong learning.

    b. What lifelong learning is and why it is growing.

    c. The best way to study in a lifelong learning course.

    d. Why lifelong learning is not as good as other kinds of learning.

According to the reading:

2. Lifelong learners were bad students when they were children.   T   F

3. Lifelong learning is too expensive for many people.   T   F

4. The number of people in lifelong learning courses is going up.   T   F

5. Most lifelong learners study something related to their job.   T   F

B Check your answers.

Score _____/5

C Summarize the key points in the reading. Turn to page 113.

Expansion Questions

1. How many years do most people in your country study?

_____

2. Do you know anyone who has continued to learn even after they finished school? Who are they? Why have they continued learning?

_____

3. Who are better learners, young people or older people? Why?

_____

Extreme Body Modification

What is beautiful?

Body modification means changing the look of the face or body, often by cutting out, coloring, or changing the shape of a person's skin. One kind of body modification, cosmetic surgery, is done to help people to look normal again. Cosmetic surgery is also for people who simply want to look more beautiful. For
5   example, these people may want to change the shape of their nose, change the shape of their eyes, or become thinner.

Most people think that everyone agrees about beauty. In other words, we believe that models and movie stars are the most beautiful, and the rest of us should try to look like them as much as possible. However, other people believe
10   that beauty means looking different from everyone else. Some may even use extreme body modification to stand out from others. For example, believers in extreme body modification may try to change their bodies so that they look very strange or look like an animal. They may use cosmetic surgery and tattoos, or they may cut body parts like their tongue or
15   fingers. They may even put things under their skin to make new shapes or add holes to their skin.

One person who is well known for his
20   extreme body modification is Erik "Lizardman" Sprague. Sprague has made himself look like a lizard by getting a full-body tattoo like green snake skin, a snake's tongue, and pointed teeth. He is
25   an artist and says that, since he doesn't hurt anyone, people should let him make his own choice to change his appearance.

Some doctors do not agree with this way of thinking. They say that this type
30   of body modification can be dangerous. They say that anyone who wants to have their body changed in this way should first go and talk to a doctor.

Time

A Circle the right answer.

1. The main idea in this reading is:

    a. What extreme body modification is.

    b. The good and bad points of tattoos.

    c. The best way to become more beautiful.

    d. Why some people choose to look different.

According to the reading:

2. Cosmetic surgery can be used to make people thinner.	T	F
3. Everyone agrees that models are beautiful.	T	F
4. Erik "Lizardman" Sprague is a waiter in a restaurant.	T	F
5. Doctors say that body modifications are fine.	T	F

B Check your answers.

Score _____ /5

C Summarize the key points in the reading. Turn to page 113.

Expansion Questions

1. Have you ever made a big change in how you look? How did it feel?

_____

2. Do you think it's better to look like other people or to look different?

_____

3. Who is the most beautiful-looking person in your opinion?

_____

Vegetarianism

Why do some people avoid eating meat?

Recent figures show that more than 375 million people in the world are vegetarian. These people do not eat the meat of any living thing. Many people go even further and do not eat things that come from animals, such as eggs and milk, or wear clothes made from animal skins. This is called veganism, and the people
5 who practice it are vegans. Being a vegan or vegetarian has become more and more common in recent years.

Although the number of vegans in the world is still quite small, there are more vegetarians than you may think. The country with the largest number of vegetarians is India. The reason for this is the Hindu religion. Hindus believe that
10 people should try not to hurt other people and animals. Its followers believe that we should not kill animals for meat, and we should not
15 keep animals to produce food like eggs and milk. Thirty-one percent of India's 1.2 billion people are vegetarians.

20 There are many reasons why people choose not to eat meat. Some people stop eating meat for health reasons. People who do
25 not eat meat live longer and are less likely to have health problems such as heart trouble and cancer. Others stop eating meat to help protect the earth. It takes more land, water, and work to take care of animals for food than it takes to grow plants, and the larger the animal, the worse it is.

30 While there are many good things about being a vegetarian, it can also be a bit difficult. Eating out can be hard, and visiting friends and family can cause problems, especially as some people do not agree with the vegetarian lifestyle. However, many people all over the world are vegetarians, and many believe that their number will continue to grow.

Time

A Circle the right answer.

1. The main idea in this reading is:

    a. Why there are few vegetarians outside of India.

    b. Why vegans are healthier than vegetarians.

    c. What vegetarianism is and why do people do it.

    d. Why Hindus don't allow vegetarianism.

According to the reading:

2. Most vegetarians in the world live in India.	T	F
3. Vegans can eat eggs and drink milk.	T	F
4. Meat can be bad for your health and the environment.	T	F
5. There are more than one billion vegetarians in the world today.	T	F

B Check your answers.

Score _____/5

C Summarize the key points in the reading. Turn to page 113.

Expansion Questions

1. In your country, do most people eat meat? What kind of meat?

_____

2. Do you know anyone who does not eat meat? Do you know why not?

_____

3. What are the good and bad points of eating meat?

_____

How Children Learn

Do we learn more easily when we are young?

Scientists used to think that people's minds did not change anymore after they were born. Now we know that children's minds actually keep changing during their first three or four years of life. That is why children learn more between ages zero and four than at any other time in their lives.

5   A young child's mind is like a computer. It is always getting and storing the information it learns, such as names, colors, and words. Even though the child cannot yet talk, they are listening to the way others speak, and the child is learning their words. Children are able to learn many different languages at this age. If they hear a language enough, they will speak that language when they begin to talk. If

10 they hear two languages, they will be able to speak both languages.

    It is interesting to think about just how much young

15 children learn. They learn how to walk and how to eat by themselves. They learn how to tell others what they want by pointing and using

20 their hands. They learn how to look at pictures and recognize family members. They learn which things are safe to touch and which things are not.

25 They learn the names of things such as "dog," "cat," "table," and "book."

    To older people, these things seem easy. This is because they cannot remember learning them. But as people get older, learning becomes more difficult. People cannot remember things as well because their minds have stopped growing. Watch a class of college students trying to learn a new language. Then watch a

30 class of young children doing the same thing. The young children may not seem to be paying attention, but the computers in their heads are always at work. These young boys and girls are learning machines.

Time

A Circle the right answer.

1. The main idea in this reading is:

    a. Children are very good at learning things.

    b. Adults can't learn new things; e.g. languages.

    c. Computers are smart and can learn like children.

    d. Children can learn two languages at once.

According to the reading:

2. Children's minds do not change after they are born.   T   F

3. Children learn to walk by watching their mothers.   T   F

4. College students should try to learn like children do.   T   F

5. Children should only study one language until the age of four.   T   F

B Check your answers.

Score _____/5

C Summarize the key points in the reading. Turn to page 113.

Expansion Questions

1. When do children start to learn? What is the first thing they learn?

_____

2. What is the earliest thing you remember learning?

_____

3. Children and adults learn languages differently. What is the difference?

_____

SUMMARIZE »»»

Summarize the key points in the readings. Include the words in the box. You can look back at the text when you do this.

33 Lifelong Learning

continuing	work	1.5 million	fun

_____

_____

_____

_____

34 Extreme Body Modification

changing	cosmetic	beauty	stand out

_____

_____

_____

_____

35 Vegetarianism

meat	veganism	reasons	difficult

_____

_____

_____

_____

36 How Children Learn

four	difficult	computer	storing

_____

_____

_____

_____

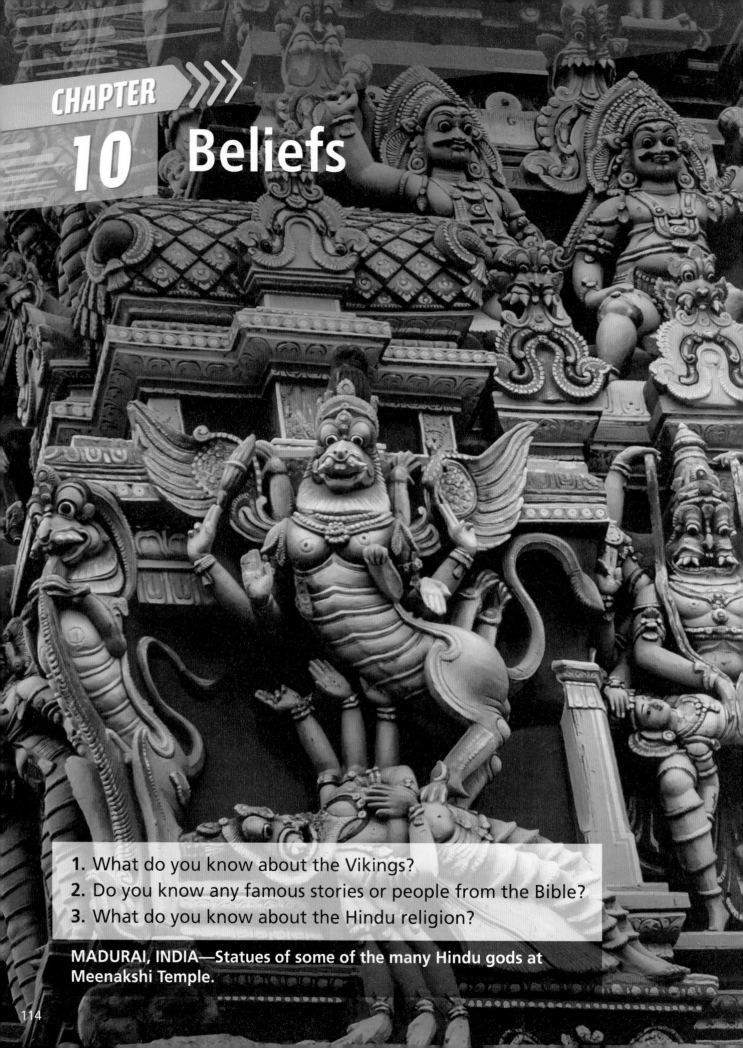

CHAPTER

10 Beliefs

1. What do you know about the Vikings?
2. Do you know any famous stories or people from the Bible?
3. What do you know about the Hindu religion?

MADURAI, INDIA—Statues of some of the many Hindu gods at Meenakshi Temple.

37 The Norse Creation Story

√	Keyword	Category	Definition	Use in a sentence
	Norse			
	religion			
	space			My bedroom is too small; I need more space.
	drop	noun		
	giant		a person or thing much larger than the usual size	
	special			
	cow			
	gods			
	skin	noun		
	Vikings			

38 Hinduism

√	Keyword	Category	Definition	Use in a sentence
	followers			
	universe			
	spiritual	adjective		
	rebirth			
	goal			
	physical			Physical things are those you can see and touch.
	communication			
	modern		not old; new	
	force	verb		
	yoga			

39 Atheism

✓	Keyword	Category	Definition	Use in a sentence
	lack		not enough of something	
	belief			
	explanation			
	develop			Babies develop inside their mother for many months.
	non-	prefix		
	earthquakes			
	tsunami			
	destroy			
	well-behaved	adjective		
	neighbor			

40 Noah's Ark

✓	Keyword	Category	Definition	Use in a sentence
	ark		an old-fashioned word for 'boat'	
	Bible			
	Christian			
	Islamic			
	Jewish			
	flood	noun		
	God	proper noun		
	promise	verb		
	violent			Punching and kicking are violent acts.
	branch		a piece of wood which grows from a larger piece	

The Norse Creation Story

What did the Vikings believe about how the world was made?

Every religion in the world has its own story of how the world was made. Perhaps one of the most interesting stories
5 comes from the old Norse religion. The Norse people believed that, before there was the earth, the sky, or any living things, there was only an empty
10 space between a world of fire and a world of ice.

In time, the fire and the ice came closer and closer together. When they finally reached each other, the fire turned the ice to water. The drops
15 from the ice fell into the empty space and became Ymir, the first of the giants. As it grew, the giant Ymir drank the milk of a special cow. Water from Ymir's body then dropped to form other giants. At the same time, the cow ate the ice, which also became water and became Buri, the first of the gods.

Buri had a son named Borr, and Borr had a son named Odin and two others.
20 Odin and his two brothers killed the giant Ymir and made the world from its body. From Ymir's skin, Odin made the land; from the blood, Odin made the sea. Odin made the trees from Ymir's hair, and the sky from the giant's head. Finally, Odin made a man and a woman and built a wall around their home, which is the earth.

Do you understand this story? If not, you are not alone. Even people who
25 study these things do not agree about the meaning. Some say that there is one important idea: that for the Norse, death is necessary to make life. If this is true, it seems like a useful way of thinking for the old Norse people, many of whom lived between worlds of ice and fire. Today we know these people as the Vikings.

Time

A Circle the right answer.

1. The main idea in this reading is:
   a. How the Norse gods created the Vikings from ice and fire.
   b. How the world, the gods, and people were created.
   c. Why death is necessary to make new life.
   d. How it is difficult to understand some creation stories.

According to the reading:

2. At first, there were only the worlds of ice and fire.   T   F
3. The giant Ymir ate the meat of a special cow.   T   F
4. Ymir then made Odin from his blood.   T   F
5. Odin and his brothers killed Ymir.   T   F

B Check your answers.

Score _____/5

C Summarize the key points in the reading. Turn to page 125.

Expansion Questions

1. What are the creation stories in your culture?

   _____

2. What do you know about the Vikings?

   _____

3. Do you know any other stories from Norse culture?

   _____

Hinduism

What is Hinduism? What do Hindus believe? Track 38

The Hindu religion is common in India and nearby countries. It is the third-largest religion in the world, with over one billion followers. It has also been called the oldest living religion in the world. It is believed that the beginning of Hinduism goes back over 3,500 years.

5 Most Hindus believe in many different gods, not only one. However, they believe that there is only one "truth," called the Brahman, which brings all things in the universe together. Some people see the Brahman as a god above the other gods, but most Hindus don't think of it as a god. They believe that the Brahman is a force which keeps the universe together.

10 Hindus follow many special books. The two most important are called the Vedas and the Upanishads. The Vedas are the stories about the gods, about the beginning of the world, and about how to live a good life. The Upanishads are about the Brahman and about how to reach spiritual freedom.

Hindus believe in a circle of birth and rebirth. This is the idea that every living 15 thing will come back again after death, maybe as another person or maybe as an animal. They also believe that there are four main goals to life: living a good life, living a meaningful life, living a physical life, and living a spiritual life. A person who can reach all of these four goals can break the circle of 20 birth and rebirth and reach spiritual freedom.

In the 1800s, Hinduism started to change as a result of British rule in India and communication with 25 the modern world. In the 1900s, many ideas from Hinduism became more and more well known in other countries. For example, the exercise known as yoga comes from 30 Hinduism and is now popular all over the world.

Time _____

A Circle the right answer.

1. The main idea in this reading is:
   a. How the universe was made.
   b. The Hindu gods.
   c. The Hindu religion.
   d. Changes in Hinduism.

According to the reading:

2. The Hindu religion is newer than most other religions.   T   F
3. Hindus do not follow any special books.   T   F
4. Hindus believe in a circle of life: birth, death, and rebirth. T   F
5. Most Hindus believe that there are many different gods.   T   F

B Check your answers.

Score _____/5

C Summarize the key points in the reading. Turn to page 125.

Expansion Questions

1. What do you know about Hinduism?
   _____

2. In what ways are Hinduism and the religion of your country different?
   _____

3. In your country's religion, what happens to people after they die?
   _____

Atheism

Why are some people not religious?

Atheism is the lack of belief in god. Atheists don't agree with religious explanations about how the world was made.
5 They want to look at things with a scientific mind and find how life developed. In other words, atheism is not a belief; it is non-belief.

10 Atheists say that when the first religions began, many thousands of years ago, people did not understand the world very well. They did not know
15 why things such as earthquakes or tsunamis happened, so people made up stories about gods. Now that people have a better understanding of the world, we do not need these old stories.

British actor Ricky Gervais, who is an atheist, has said: "If we took any religious book and destroyed it, in a thousand years it wouldn't come back just as
20 it was. But if we took every science book and destroyed them, those facts would all be back. Science would make all the same discoveries again." Gervais thinks this is how we can know that science is true.

Most atheists do not want to stop religion. They know that many people believe in religion and this makes them feel better. However, atheists do believe
25 that no one should be pushed toward a religion. They do not want religion to be part of law or government.

One of their ideas is that religion does not seem to make people act better. For example, Japan—a country where most people are non-religious—is known for low crime rates and well-behaved people. On the other hand, many religious
30 countries have much higher crime rates.

Most atheists agree with religious ideas such as "Love your neighbor as yourself." They think that stories in religious books are often beautiful and helpful to think about. Where they don't agree is that these stories are fact.

Time

A Circle the right answer.

1. The main idea in this reading is:
   a. How religion is wrong.
   b. How atheists have suffered.
   c. The effects of atheism on behavior.
   d. What atheism is.

According to the reading:

2. Thousands of years ago, most people were atheists.   T   F
3. Ricky Gervais said we should "love our neighbor."   T   F
4. Atheists want to push people to believe in science.   T   F
5. Atheist countries have more crime than other countries.   T   F

B Check your answers.

Score _____/5

C Summarize the key points in the reading. Turn to page 125.

Expansion Questions

1. Are there many atheists in your country?

   _____

2. How do atheists explain the origin of life?

   _____

3. In some countries, it is dangerous to be an atheist. Why?

   _____

Noah's Ark

What is this famous story, and what does it mean?

Noah's Ark is one of the best-known stories in the Bible. It is an important story in Christian, Islamic, and Jewish religions. The story tells of a great flood which kills all people on earth except for one family chosen by God. This great flood covered the whole world to the top of the highest mountain.

5   In the story, God is unhappy with the people he has made because they have become bad and violent. One day, God appears to the only good man, Noah, and tells him that he will soon clear the earth by flooding it. He says to

10   Noah, "Build a great boat— an ark—and fill it with two of each animal, one male and one female. When it starts to rain, get in the ark

15   with your family. You will be saved, but everyone else will die."

Noah and his sons built the great ark as God had

20   asked them. While they worked, everyone else laughed. They said that Noah was crazy for building a boat on dry land. However, when the ark was complete and filled with animals, it started to rain. Soon the whole world was under water. Everyone but Noah and his family died.

25   After forty days and forty nights, the rain stopped. Noah sent out a bird to see if it could find land. Many days passed. One day, the bird came back with a small green branch. Noah knew that the water was going down. Soon they could see dry land, and God told Noah to let the animals out. Then God promised Noah that he would never send a flood like that again.

30   Although there is no sign of a flood which covered the whole world, it is interesting that many other cultures also tell stories of a great flood.

Time

A Circle the right answer.

1. The main idea in this reading is:

a. Keeping animals alive.

b. The building of Noah's ark.

c. The story of Noah's ark.

d. The danger of flood.

According to the reading:

2. Noah's Ark is only a Christian story.	T	F
3. God told Noah to bring only good animals into the ark.	T	F
4. People laughed at Noah and his children.	T	F
5. There is no sign that a worldwide flood ever happened.	T	F

B Check your answers.

Score _____ /5

C Summarize the key points in the reading. Turn to page 125.

Expansion Questions

1. If we suddenly had to save all of the world's animals, how could we do it?

_____

2. If Noah's God looked at the world today, would he be happy or unhappy?

_____

3. There is a collection of seeds in a safe place in Norway called the Svalbard Global Seed Vault. Why?

_____

SUMMARIZE

Summarize the key points in the readings. Include the words in the box. You can look back at the text when you do this.

37 The Norse Creation Story

world	fire and ice	giants	Odin

_____

_____

_____

_____

38 Hinduism

one billion	gods	books	circle

_____

_____

_____

_____

39 Atheism

lack	understanding	pushed	well-behaved

_____

_____

_____

_____

40 Noah's Ark

best-known	unhappy	boat	branch

_____

_____

_____

_____

READING SPEED CHART

Write your score for each reading passage at the bottom of the chart. Then put an X in one of the boxes above the reading passage number to mark your time for each passage. Look on the right side of the chart to find your reading speed for each reading passage.

TIME	1	2	3	4	5	6	7	8	9	10	11	12	13	14	15	16	17	18	19	20	WPM
1 m 10 s																					257
1 m 15 s																					240
1 m 20 s																					225
1 m 25 s																					212
1 m 30 s																					200
1 m 35 s																					189
1 m 40 s																					180
1 m 45 s																					171
1 m 50 s																					164
1 m 55 s																					157
2 m 0 s																					150
2 m 5 s																					144
2 m 10 s																					138
2 m 15 s																					133
2 m 20 s																					129
2 m 25 s																					124
2 m 30 s																					120
2 m 35 s																					116
2 m 40 s																					113
2 m 45 s																					109
2 m 50 s																					106
2 m 55 s																					103
3 m 0 s																					100
3 m 5 m																					97
3 m 10 s																					95
READING	1	2	3	4	5	6	7	8	9	10	11	12	13	14	15	16	17	18	19	20	
SCORE																					

READING SPEED CHART

Write your score for each reading passage at the bottom of the chart. Then put an X in one of the boxes above the reading passage number to mark your time for each passage. Look on the right side of the chart to find your reading speed for each reading passage.

TIME	21	22	23	24	25	26	27	28	29	30	31	32	33	34	35	36	37	38	39	40	WPM
1 m 10 s																					257
1 m 15 s																					240
1 m 20 s																					225
1 m 25 s																					212
1 m 30 s																					200
1 m 35 s																					189
1 m 40 s																					180
1 m 45 s																					171
1 m 50 s																					164
1 m 55 s																					157
2 m 0 s																					150
2 m 5 s																					144
2 m 10 s																					138
2 m 15 s																					133
2 m 20 s																					129
2 m 25 s																					124
2 m 30 s																					120
2 m 35 s																					116
2 m 40 s																					113
2 m 45 s																					109
2 m 50 s																					106
2 m 55 s																					103
3 m 0 s																					100
3 m 5 m																					97
3 m 10 s																					95
READING	21	22	23	24	25	26	27	28	29	30	31	32	33	34	35	36	37	38	39	40	
SCORE																					